Table Of Contents

Chapter 1: Introduction to Holiday Delights

The Joy of Holiday Baking

The holiday season is a time filled with warmth, love, and delicious treats. One of the most beloved traditions during this time of year is holiday baking. The aroma of freshly baked cookies, pies, and cakes fills the air, creating a sense of joy and anticipation. In our book, "Holiday Delights: Family-Favorite Treats and Classic Cheesecake Recipes," we invite you to experience the joy of holiday baking and create lasting memories with your loved ones.

For anyone, family, and all those who cherish family-favorite holiday treats, this subchapter is a treasure trove of timeless cheesecake and dessert recipes that will surely become a part of your holiday traditions. From classic gingerbread cookies to decadent chocolate cakes, we have gathered an array of recipes that will delight your taste buds and impress your guests.

Baking together as a family is a wonderful way to bond and create cherished memories. Whether you have little ones eagerly rolling dough or teenagers perfecting their piping skills, holiday baking is an activity that brings everyone together. From the youngest to the oldest, everyone can be a part of the joy and excitement that fills the kitchen.

In this subchapter, we provide step-by-step instructions and helpful tips for each recipe, ensuring that even novice bakers can successfully create these delightful treats. From the traditional to the unique, our recipes cater to a variety of tastes and dietary restrictions. Whether you prefer a classic New York-style cheesecake or a vegan-friendly pumpkin pie, we have something for everyone.

The holiday season is a time for indulgence, and what better way to indulge than with a slice of rich, creamy cheesecake or a batch of freshly baked cookies? The satisfaction of creating something delicious from scratch and sharing it with your loved ones is truly unmatched. As you gather around the table, savoring each bite, you will feel the joy and love that went into every recipe.

So, dust off your aprons, gather your ingredients, and get ready to embark on a delightful baking journey. Let the sweet aromas fill your home and the warmth of the oven bring comfort to your heart. With our book, "Holiday Delights: Family-Favorite Treats and Classic Cheesecake Recipes," you can create lasting memories and delicious treats that will be cherished for years to come.

Chapter 1: Introduction to Holiday Delights

The Joy of Holiday Baking

The holiday season is a time filled with warmth, love, and delicious treats. One of the most beloved traditions during this time of year is holiday baking. The aroma of freshly baked cookies, pies, and cakes fills the air, creating a sense of joy and anticipation. In our book, "Holiday Delights: Family-Favorite Treats and Classic Cheesecake Recipes," we invite you to experience the joy of holiday baking and create lasting memories with your loved ones.

For anyone, family, and all those who cherish family-favorite holiday treats, this subchapter is a treasure trove of timeless cheesecake and dessert recipes that will surely become a part of your holiday traditions. From classic gingerbread cookies to decadent chocolate cakes, we have gathered an array of recipes that will delight your taste buds and impress your guests.

Baking together as a family is a wonderful way to bond and create cherished memories. Whether you have little ones eagerly rolling dough or teenagers perfecting their piping skills, holiday baking is an activity that brings everyone together. From the youngest to the oldest, everyone can be a part of the joy and excitement that fills the kitchen.

In this subchapter, we provide step-by-step instructions and helpful tips for each recipe, ensuring that even novice bakers can successfully create these delightful treats. From the traditional to the unique, our recipes cater to a variety of tastes and dietary restrictions. Whether you prefer a classic New York-style cheesecake or a vegan-friendly pumpkin pie, we have something for everyone.

The holiday season is a time for indulgence, and what better way to indulge than with a slice of rich, creamy cheesecake or a batch of freshly baked cookies? The satisfaction of creating something delicious from scratch and sharing it with your loved ones is truly unmatched. As you gather around the table, savoring each bite, you will feel the joy and love that went into every recipe.

So, dust off your aprons, gather your ingredients, and get ready to embark on a delightful baking journey. Let the sweet aromas fill your home and the warmth of the oven bring comfort to your heart. With our book, "Holiday Delights: Family-Favorite Treats and Classic Cheesecake Recipes," you can create lasting memories and delicious treats that will be cherished for years to come.

Importance of Family-Favorite Treats

In our fast-paced and ever-evolving world, it is easy to get caught up in the hustle and bustle of life. However, amidst the chaos, there is one thing that remains constant and timeless - the importance of family-favorite treats. These delightful culinary creations not only bring joy and satisfaction to our taste buds but also hold a special place in our hearts.

Family-favorite treats have a unique ability to transport us back in time, evoking cherished memories and creating a sense of nostalgia. Whether it's grandma's famous apple pie or mom's secret recipe for chocolate chip cookies, these treats have the power to connect us with our past and make us feel truly at home. They remind us of the love and care that went into preparing them, and the joyous moments we shared with our loved ones.

Moreover, family-favorite treats play a significant role in strengthening the bonds within a family. When we gather around the table to enjoy these scrumptious delights, we create an atmosphere of togetherness and unity. The process of baking and cooking together fosters teamwork and collaboration, allowing family members to share their skills and knowledge. It is during these moments that stories are shared, traditions are passed down, and laughter fills the air. The act of preparing and sharing these treats becomes a cherished family ritual, creating lasting memories that will be treasured for years to come.

Family-favorite treats also hold a unique significance during the holiday season. These festive delicacies are an integral part of our holiday traditions, bringing warmth and joy to our celebrations. Whether it's gingerbread cookies during Christmas or pumpkin pie on Thanksgiving, these treats symbolize the spirit of the season and create a sense of anticipation and excitement. They add a touch of magic to our festivities and serve as a reminder of the importance of coming together as a family during these special times.

In "Holiday Delights: Family-Favorite Treats and Classic Cheesecake Recipes," you will discover a collection of timeless recipes that have been passed down through generations. From delectable holiday treats to classic cheesecake recipes, this book is a treasure trove of culinary delights that are sure to become your family's favorites.

So, gather your loved ones, put on your aprons, and embark on a journey through these delightful recipes. Create memories, share stories, and indulge in the magic of family-favorite treats. Because, at the end of the day, it is these simple pleasures that truly make life worth living.

Exploring the Timeless Appeal of Cheesecakes

Cheesecakes have been a beloved dessert for centuries, captivating the hearts and taste buds of people from all walks of life. In "Holiday Delights: Family-Favorite Treats and Classic Cheesecake Recipes," we delve into the timeless appeal of these delectable desserts that have become a staple on family tables during holidays and special occasions.

There is something magical about the creamy, velvety texture and rich, indulgent flavor of a perfectly made cheesecake. It is a dessert that transcends time and generations, leaving a lasting impression on anyone who takes a bite. Whether it is a classic New York-style cheesecake or a creative twist with unique flavors and toppings, cheesecakes have a way of bringing joy and satisfaction to those who savor them.

One of the reasons why cheesecakes have stood the test of time is their versatility. With countless variations and flavors to choose from, cheesecakes can be customized to suit any occasion or preference. From traditional favorites like strawberry, blueberry, and chocolate to more adventurous combinations like salted caramel, pumpkin spice, and even savory options, there is a cheesecake for every palate.

Furthermore, cheesecakes are not only delicious but also visually appealing. Their smooth, glossy surfaces and decorative toppings make them a feast for the eyes as well as the taste buds. Whether it's a simple dusting of powdered sugar, a drizzle of chocolate ganache, or an artful arrangement of fresh fruits, cheesecakes are a stunning centerpiece that adds elegance and charm to any dessert table.

Moreover, cheesecakes have a comforting and nostalgic quality that resonates with families. Many of us have fond memories of enjoying cheesecake with our loved ones during holidays and family gatherings. The act of sharing a slice of cheesecake can create a sense of togetherness and warmth, making it the perfect dessert for celebrations and creating lasting family traditions.

In this subchapter of "Holiday Delights: Family-Favorite Treats and Classic Cheesecake Recipes," we will embark on a journey to explore the timeless appeal of cheesecakes. From the history and origins of these heavenly desserts to tips and techniques for mastering the perfect cheesecake, we will provide you with a comprehensive guide to creating memorable cheesecake experiences for your family.

So, whether you are a seasoned cheesecake enthusiast or just discovering the joys of this timeless dessert, join us on this delightful adventure as we celebrate the magic and timelessness of cheesecakes. Let the aroma of creamy goodness fill your kitchen and the taste transport you to a world of sweet bliss. Get ready to indulge in the enchanting world of cheesecakes and create treasured moments with your loved ones that will be cherished for years to come.

Overview of Classic Dessert Recipes

In this subchapter, we will explore the delightful world of classic dessert recipes. From decadent cakes to mouthwatering pies, these recipes have stood the test of time and continue to be cherished by families around the world.

Classic desserts hold a special place in our hearts, as they are often associated with fond memories and cherished traditions. Whether it's a special occasion or a simple family gathering, these timeless treats never fail to bring joy and happiness to the table.

One of the all-time favorites among classic desserts is the traditional apple pie. The combination of sweet, tart apples, warm spices, and buttery crust creates a heavenly aroma that fills the house. Serve it warm with a scoop of vanilla ice cream, and you have the perfect ending to any meal.

Another beloved classic is the rich and creamy chocolate cake. This indulgent dessert is a crowd-pleaser, and its velvety texture and intense chocolate flavor make it a true showstopper. Whether you prefer a simple, moist chocolate cake or a layered masterpiece, there's no denying the irresistible allure of this timeless treat.

For those with a sweet tooth, no classic dessert list would be complete without the mention of homemade cookies. From chewy chocolate chip cookies to delicate sugar cookies, these baked goodies are a staple in every household. Baking a batch of cookies with your loved ones is not only a delicious experience but also a wonderful opportunity to bond and create lasting memories.

Lastly, we cannot forget the classic cheesecake. With its smooth and creamy texture, this dessert has been a favorite for generations. From the traditional New York-style cheesecake to fruity variations like strawberry or blueberry, there's a cheesecake recipe to suit every taste.

In this subchapter, we will provide detailed recipes and step-by-step instructions for each classic dessert mentioned. We will also share some tips and tricks to ensure your desserts turn out perfectly every time. Whether you're a seasoned baker or a beginner, these recipes are sure to impress your family and loved ones.

So, grab your apron and get ready to embark on a delicious journey through the world of classic desserts. These recipes have been handed down through generations, and it's time to create your own family traditions with these timeless treats.

Chapter 2: Family-Favorite Holiday Treats

Traditional Christmas Cookies

Christmas is a time for joy, love, and of course, delicious treats! And what better way to celebrate the holiday season than with a batch of homemade traditional Christmas cookies? These timeless delights have been a part of holiday traditions for generations, bringing warmth and comfort to families around the world.

In this subchapter, we will explore some of the most beloved traditional Christmas cookie recipes that are sure to become family favorites. From classic sugar cookies to gingerbread men, these treats capture the essence of the holiday season.

First on our list is the sugar cookie, a staple in every Christmas cookie jar. These buttery delights are adorned with colorful icing and festive sprinkles, making them a fun and delicious activity for the whole family. Whether you cut them into traditional shapes like stars and bells or let your imagination run wild, sugar cookies are a must-have during the holidays.

Next up, we have the classic gingerbread cookies. These spiced delights not only fill your home with the irresistible aroma of cinnamon and cloves but also bring back memories of decorating gingerbread houses and making gingerbread men. With their charming shapes and rich flavors, gingerbread cookies are a true delight for young and old alike.

If you're looking for a twist on tradition, try baking a batch of peppermint chocolate cookies. The combination of rich chocolate and refreshing peppermint creates a mouthwatering treat that screams holiday cheer. Whether you choose to enjoy them with a cup of hot cocoa or share them with friends and family, these cookies are sure to become a new holiday favorite.

Finally, no Christmas cookie collection would be complete without the classic shortbread cookie. With its buttery and crumbly texture, this simple yet elegant treat is perfect for enjoying with a hot cup of tea or coffee. Decorate them with a sprinkle of powdered sugar or dip them in melted chocolate for an extra indulgence.

Whether you're a seasoned baker or just starting, these traditional Christmas cookies are sure to bring joy and happiness to your holiday season. So gather your loved ones, put on some holiday tunes, and let the baking begin!

Sugar Cookies with Festive Decorations

Sugar cookies with festive decorations are a delightful addition to any holiday celebration. Whether you are planning a family gathering, a holiday party, or simply want to indulge in some seasonal treats, these cookies are sure to please everyone. In this subchapter, we will explore the art of making sugar cookies from scratch and adding festive decorations to make them truly special.

The first step in creating these delicious cookies is to gather all the necessary ingredients. You will need flour, sugar, butter, eggs, vanilla extract, salt, and baking powder. Once you have all the ingredients, it's time to start baking. The recipe in this book will guide you through the process, ensuring that your cookies turn out soft, chewy, and full of flavor.

Once the cookies are baked and cooled, it's time to decorate them. This is where the fun begins! You can let your creativity shine by using various decorations such as colorful icing, sprinkles, and edible glitter. Let the kids join in the fun by letting them decorate their own cookies. It's a great way to spend quality time together as a family and create lasting memories.

To make the cookies even more festive, consider using cookie cutters in holiday shapes like Christmas trees, snowflakes, or gingerbread men. You can also use food coloring in the icing to create vibrant and eye-catching designs. The possibilities are endless when it comes to decorating sugar cookies, so let your imagination run wild.

These sugar cookies with festive decorations are not only delicious but also make for a beautiful presentation. Arrange them on a decorative platter or wrap them in festive packaging to give as gifts. They are sure to be a hit at any holiday gathering and will leave everyone asking for the recipe.

In conclusion, sugar cookies with festive decorations are a must-have for any holiday celebration. They are a classic treat that brings joy and happiness to everyone who takes a bite. Get creative, involve the whole family, and let your imagination run wild with the decorations. The end result will be a plate full of delicious cookies that will become a family-favorite holiday treat for years to come.

Gingerbread People and Houses

One of the most beloved holiday traditions for families all around the world is the making and decorating of gingerbread people and houses. These delightful treats not only fill the air with the warm and spicy aroma of cinnamon and ginger but also bring families together in the spirit of creativity and holiday cheer.

Gingerbread people are fun and easy to make, and they provide a perfect canvas for the imagination. Gather your loved ones in the kitchen, put on some festive music, and let the holiday magic begin. Start by mixing together flour, baking soda, ginger, cinnamon, cloves, and a pinch of salt. In a separate bowl, cream together butter and brown sugar until light and fluffy, then add molasses and an egg. Slowly incorporate the dry ingredients into the wet mixture until a smooth dough forms. Chill the dough for at least an hour before rolling it out and cutting it into the desired shapes.

Once the gingerbread people are baked and cooled, it's time for the real fun to begin – decorating! Set up a decorating station with an array of colorful icing, sprinkles, and candies. Let your creativity run wild as you give each gingerbread person a unique personality. Perhaps one will have a fancy hat, while another will wear a polka dot dress. The possibilities are endless, and the smiles and laughter are guaranteed.

If you're feeling extra ambitious, why not take gingerbread creations to the next level and build a gingerbread house? The process is similar to making gingerbread people, but you will need to create templates for the walls, roof, and other components of the house. Once the gingerbread pieces are baked and cooled, use royal icing as glue to assemble the house. Decorate it with candies, pretzels, and other edible delights, turning it into a whimsical and delicious masterpiece.

Gingerbread people and houses are not only delightful treats but also treasured family keepsakes. They can be hung on the Christmas tree or displayed on a festive platter, adding a touch of holiday magic to your home decor. So, gather your loved ones this holiday season and create memories that will last a lifetime with these classic gingerbread treats. Spread the joy and share the love as you indulge in these family-favorite holiday delights.

Peppermint Candy Cane Cookies

If there's one thing that instantly brings the holiday spirit to life, it's the delightful aroma of freshly baked cookies wafting through the house. And when those cookies are infused with the refreshing taste of peppermint and adorned with candy cane pieces, it's a treat that is sure to please the entire family. In this subchapter, we present to you our beloved recipe for Peppermint Candy Cane Cookies – a holiday delight that will become a family-favorite in no time.

The allure of these cookies lies not only in their festive appearance but also in their irresistible flavor combination. The buttery, melt-in-your-mouth texture of the cookie dough is perfectly complemented by the cool, minty essence of peppermint. As you take a bite, your taste buds will revel in the harmonious blend of sweet and refreshing notes, leaving you craving for more.

Preparing these Peppermint Candy Cane Cookies is an enjoyable activity that the whole family can partake in. From measuring and mixing the ingredients to forming the dough into candy cane shapes, everyone can contribute to the creation of these delightful treats. The process is not only a chance for family bonding but also an opportunity to pass down cherished holiday traditions from one generation to the next.

Once the cookies are baked to golden perfection, it's time for the final touch – the candy cane toppings. Crushed candy cane pieces are carefully sprinkled over the cookies, adding a festive flair and a satisfying crunch with every bite. These cookies are not only a delight for the taste buds but also a visual treat that embodies the essence of the holiday season.

Whether you're planning a holiday gathering or simply want to indulge in a cozy evening with your loved ones, our Peppermint Candy Cane Cookies are the perfect accompaniment. They can be savored alongside a cup of hot cocoa or paired with a scoop of vanilla ice cream for a decadent dessert. No matter how you choose to enjoy them, these cookies are guaranteed to spread joy and create lasting memories for your family.

So, gather your loved ones, put on some holiday music, and embark on a baking adventure that will fill your home with the warmth and aroma of the season. With our Peppermint Candy Cane Cookies recipe, you're bound to create an irresistible treat that will become a family-favorite for years to come. Happy baking, and happy holidays!

Decadent Thanksgiving Pies

Thanksgiving is a time for indulgence, and what better way to satisfy your sweet tooth than with a delectable pie? In this subchapter, we will explore the world of decadent Thanksgiving pies that are sure to become family favorites. From classic flavors to unique twists, these pies will add an extra touch of delight to your holiday feast.

First on the list is the all-time favorite, pumpkin pie. This velvety smooth pie with a perfectly spiced filling is a must-have on Thanksgiving. It's a timeless dessert that brings back childhood memories and warms the heart. Our recipe includes a flaky, homemade crust that complements the rich pumpkin filling beautifully.

For those looking for something a little different, try our caramel apple pie. The combination of tart apples, sweet caramel, and a buttery crust creates a heavenly treat that will leave everyone wanting seconds. Topped with a scoop of vanilla ice cream, this pie is pure heaven.

If you're a fan of pecan pie, you're in for a treat. Our version takes this classic dessert to the next level by adding a touch of bourbon. The result is a deep, rich flavor that will have your taste buds dancing. The crunchy pecans and gooey filling make this pie an irresistible Thanksgiving indulgence.

For chocolate lovers, our triple chocolate silk pie is a showstopper. With layers of silky smooth chocolate mousse, rich ganache, and a chocolate cookie crust, this pie is pure decadence. It's the perfect ending to a Thanksgiving feast and will impress even the most discerning dessert connoisseurs.

Last but not least, we have a twist on the traditional sweet potato pie. Our recipe adds a hint of cinnamon and nutmeg to the sweet potato filling, creating a warm and comforting pie that captures the essence of fall. Topped with a dollop of whipped cream, this pie is sure to be a hit with the whole family.

Whether you stick to the classics or venture into more adventurous flavors, these decadent Thanksgiving pies will elevate your holiday feast to new heights. With their rich flavors, flaky crusts, and irresistible fillings, they are guaranteed to become family favorites for years to come. So this Thanksgiving, treat yourself and your loved ones to a slice of pure indulgence with these delightful pies.

Classic Pumpkin Pie with Whipped Cream

There's nothing quite like the comforting aroma of a freshly baked pumpkin pie wafting through the house during the holiday season. This timeless dessert has been a family-favorite for generations and remains a beloved treat on Thanksgiving and Christmas tables across the country. In this subchapter, we will explore the classic recipe for pumpkin pie, accompanied by a luscious dollop of homemade whipped cream.

To start, gather the essential ingredients: a pre-made or homemade pie crust, canned pumpkin puree, eggs, sugar, cinnamon, nutmeg, ginger, cloves, salt, and evaporated milk. The pie crust provides a buttery and flaky base for the rich pumpkin filling, while the combination of aromatic spices adds warmth and depth to the dessert.

Begin by preheating the oven to 425°F (220°C). Roll out the pie crust and fit it into a pie dish, crimping the edges for a decorative touch. In a large mixing bowl, whisk together the pumpkin puree, eggs, sugar, spices, and salt until well combined. Slowly pour in the evaporated milk while continuing to whisk until the filling is smooth and velvety.

Next, carefully pour the pumpkin filling into the prepared pie crust, ensuring an even distribution. Place the pie in the preheated oven and bake for 15 minutes. Then, reduce the oven temperature to 350°F (175°C) and continue baking for an additional 40-50 minutes, or until the center is set.

While the pie bakes, let's prepare the whipped cream topping. In a chilled mixing bowl, combine heavy cream, powdered sugar, and vanilla extract. Using an electric mixer, beat the mixture on high speed until stiff peaks form. This airy and sweet whipped cream will complement the spiced pumpkin pie perfectly.

Once the pie is done baking, remove it from the oven and allow it to cool completely before serving. To serve, cut generous slices of the pumpkin pie and top each piece with a dollop of the homemade whipped cream. The creamy, smooth texture of the pie filling combined with the fluffy whipped cream creates a delightful contrast that will satisfy every sweet tooth at the table.

Whether enjoyed at a holiday gathering or as a special treat for your family, this classic pumpkin pie with whipped cream is sure to be a hit. Its timeless flavors and comforting appeal make it a cherished dessert for all ages. So gather your loved ones, savor the flavors of the season, and indulge in this festive delight that will make your holidays even more memorable.

Pecan Pie with a Buttery Crust

Pecan pie is a classic dessert that is often associated with holiday gatherings and family traditions. The sweet, gooey filling combined with the crunchy pecans creates a delightful flavor and texture that is hard to resist. And when paired with a buttery crust, it takes this dessert to a whole new level of deliciousness.

In this chapter, we will explore the art of making the perfect pecan pie with a buttery crust. We will share a tried and true recipe that has been passed down through generations, ensuring that your family will be able to enjoy this scrumptious treat for years to come.

To start, let's talk about the crust. A buttery crust adds a richness and depth of flavor to the pecan pie. The key is to use cold butter and cut it into the flour mixture until it resembles coarse crumbs. This will create a flaky and tender crust that will perfectly complement the sweet filling.

Next, let's dive into the filling. Traditional pecan pie filling consists of a mixture of eggs, sugar, corn syrup, vanilla extract, and of course, pecans. The combination of these ingredients creates a gooey and sweet filling that is simply irresistible. The pecans add a nutty and crunchy element that balances out the sweetness, making each bite a delight for your taste buds.

Once you have prepared the crust and the filling, it's time to assemble the pie. Gently pour the filling into the prepared crust, making sure to distribute the pecans evenly. Carefully place the pie in the oven and let it bake until the filling is set and the crust is golden brown.

As the pie bakes, your kitchen will be filled with the warm and inviting aroma of pecans and buttery crust. The anticipation will build as you eagerly wait for the pie to cool down before slicing into it. When the time finally comes, you will be rewarded with a slice of pecan pie that is bursting with flavor and nostalgia.

Whether you're hosting a holiday gathering or simply craving a sweet treat, pecan pie with a buttery crust is a timeless dessert that will never disappoint. So grab a slice, gather your loved ones, and create lasting memories as you indulge in this family-favorite holiday delight.

Apple Pie with a Cinnamon Streusel Topping

There is no better way to celebrate the holiday season than with a warm and delicious apple pie. And when it comes to apple pies, nothing beats the classic combination of sweet apples and a buttery, cinnamon streusel topping. In this subchapter, we will explore the step-by-step process of making an irresistible apple pie with a cinnamon streusel topping that will surely become a family favorite.

To begin, gather all the ingredients needed for the pie crust, including flour, butter, sugar, and salt. Follow the instructions provided to make a flaky and tender crust that will serve as the perfect base for the apple filling.

Next, it's time to prepare the apple filling. Choose a variety of apples such as Granny Smith, Honeycrisp, or Gala for a balanced blend of tartness and sweetness. Peel, core, and slice the apples, then toss them with cinnamon, sugar, and a touch of lemon juice. This will ensure that the apples are perfectly seasoned and will result in a vibrant and flavorful filling.

Once the crust and filling are ready, assemble the pie by placing the apple filling into the pie crust. Now, it's time to prepare the star of the show – the cinnamon streusel topping. In a separate bowl, combine flour, brown sugar, cinnamon, and butter, and mix until crumbly. Sprinkle this streusel mixture generously over the apple filling, covering it completely.

Now, it's time to bake the pie to golden perfection. Place the pie in a preheated oven and let it bake until the crust is golden brown and the filling is bubbling. The aroma of cinnamon and apples will fill your kitchen, creating an irresistible anticipation for the final result.

Once the pie is baked, allow it to cool slightly before serving. For an extra touch of indulgence, serve the apple pie warm with a scoop of vanilla ice cream or a dollop of freshly whipped cream.

This apple pie with a cinnamon streusel topping is a timeless dessert that will bring joy and warmth to your family gatherings during the holiday season. The combination of sweet and tart apples, warm cinnamon, and buttery streusel creates a symphony of flavors that will leave everyone craving for more. So gather your loved ones, roll up your sleeves, and get ready to create a holiday delight that will become a family tradition for years to come.

Festive Valentine's Day Sweets

Valentine's Day is a special time to celebrate love and affection for our loved ones. And what better way to express our feelings than with delicious, homemade sweets? In this subchapter, we dive into the world of Festive Valentine's Day Sweets that will surely delight anyone in your family.

The beauty of these treats lies not only in their delectable taste but also in the joy of making them together with your loved ones. Whether you are a seasoned baker or just starting out, these easy-to-follow recipes are perfect for creating cherished memories with your family.

Indulge in the classic favorite, chocolate-covered strawberries. This timeless treat is a staple for Valentine's Day celebrations. Dip fresh, juicy strawberries into melted chocolate, and let them set before serving. The combination of the sweet, tangy fruit and rich, smooth chocolate is simply irresistible.

For a twist on the traditional, try making heart-shaped sugar cookies. Roll out the dough and use heart-shaped cookie cutters to create adorable cookies. Decorate them with pink and red icing and sprinkle them with colorful candy hearts. These cookies are not only delicious but also make for a lovely edible gift.

If you're feeling adventurous, why not try making homemade truffles? These bite-sized delights are surprisingly easy to make. Combine melted chocolate with heavy cream and roll the mixture into small balls. Coat them in cocoa powder or dip them in melted white chocolate for an elegant touch. These decadent treats are perfect for sharing with loved ones or as a special surprise for your significant other.

Lastly, no Valentine's Day celebration is complete without a luscious cheesecake. Our book includes a collection of timeless cheesecake recipes that will surely become family favorites. From classic New York-style cheesecakes to fruity variations like raspberry swirl and strawberry shortcake, there's a cheesecake for every palate.

Whether you're looking to impress your loved ones or simply want to treat yourself, these Festive Valentine's Day Sweets are guaranteed to make your celebrations extra special. So gather your family, put on some music, and let the magic of baking bring you closer together.

Heart-Shaped Chocolate Truffles

If you're looking for a classic yet indulgent treat to make for your family and loved ones during the holidays, look no further than heart-shaped chocolate truffles. These delectable bite-sized delights are a perfect way to show your affection and satisfy your sweet tooth.

Making heart-shaped chocolate truffles is a fun and enjoyable activity that the whole family can participate in. With simple ingredients and easy-to-follow steps, you'll have a batch of these irresistible treats in no time. Plus, they make a great homemade gift that is sure to bring a smile to anyone's face.

To start, gather the necessary ingredients: high-quality dark chocolate, heavy cream, butter, and optional flavorings such as vanilla extract or liqueur. You can also add toppings like cocoa powder, crushed nuts, or sprinkles to enhance the truffles' appearance and taste.

The first step is to melt the chocolate and butter together, either using a double boiler or a microwave. Be sure to stir occasionally to ensure a smooth and velvety texture. Once melted, add the cream and any flavorings you desire. Mix everything until well combined, and then let the mixture cool to room temperature.

Once the mixture has cooled, it's time to shape the truffles into hearts. You can use a heart-shaped cookie cutter or simply roll the mixture into small balls and then shape them into hearts with your hands. Place the shaped truffles on a baking sheet lined with parchment paper and refrigerate for at least an hour to allow them to firm up.

After chilling, your heart-shaped chocolate truffles are ready to be enjoyed! Dust them with cocoa powder or roll them in your favorite toppings for added flavor and charm. These truffles can be stored in an airtight container in the refrigerator for up to two weeks, making them the perfect make-ahead treat for holiday gatherings or gifting.

Whether you're looking to impress your family or surprise your loved ones, heart-shaped chocolate truffles are a delightful addition to any holiday spread. Their rich and creamy texture, combined with the sweetness of chocolate, will undoubtedly leave everyone wanting more. So, gather your loved ones, roll up your sleeves, and get ready to create these irresistible treats that will bring joy and happiness to all.

Strawberry Shortcake with Fresh Whipped Cream

One of the most beloved desserts during the holiday season is the classic Strawberry Shortcake with Fresh Whipped Cream. This timeless treat is always a hit with anyone, whether it's enjoyed with family or friends. The combination of sweet strawberries, fluffy cake, and creamy whipped cream creates a delightful dessert that is both light and satisfying.

To make this family-favorite dessert, you will need a few simple ingredients. Start by gathering fresh strawberries, preferably ripe and juicy. Wash and slice them, then sprinkle some sugar to bring out their natural sweetness. Set them aside to let the flavors meld together.

Next, prepare the cake base. You can opt for a store-bought sponge cake or make one from scratch using a simple recipe. The key is to keep the cake light and airy, as it will absorb the flavors of the strawberries and cream perfectly. Once the cake is cooled, cut it into individual serving sizes.

Now, it's time to whip up the star of the show – the fresh whipped cream. There is nothing quite like the taste and texture of homemade whipped cream. Simply whisk together heavy cream, powdered sugar, and a splash of vanilla extract until soft peaks form. Be careful not to over-whip, as you want the cream to be light and billowy.

To assemble the strawberry shortcakes, place a layer of cake at the bottom of each serving dish. Spoon a generous amount of strawberries on top, allowing their sweet juices to soak into the cake. Finish it off with a dollop of fresh whipped cream, and perhaps a sprig of mint for a touch of freshness.

The result is a dessert that is both visually stunning and incredibly delicious. Each bite is a delightful combination of the tartness from the strawberries, the sweetness from the cake, and the light creaminess from the whipped cream. It's a dessert that never fails to bring smiles to faces and leaves everyone wanting more.

Whether enjoyed during a holiday gathering or as a special treat for the family, Strawberry Shortcake with Fresh Whipped Cream is a true crowd-pleaser. Its simplicity and timeless appeal make it a perfect addition to any dessert table, and it will surely become a family favorite for years to come.

Red Velvet Cupcakes with Cream Cheese Frosting

Red Velvet cupcakes are a classic and beloved treat that are perfect for any occasion, but especially during the holiday season. These moist and decadent cupcakes are topped with a rich and tangy cream cheese frosting that perfectly complements the subtle cocoa flavor of the cake. In this subchapter, we will explore the step-by-step process of baking these delightful cupcakes and creating a luscious cream cheese frosting.

To start, gather all the necessary ingredients, including all-purpose flour, cocoa powder, baking soda, salt, unsalted butter, granulated sugar, eggs, buttermilk, vanilla extract, red food coloring, and distilled white vinegar. These ingredients are commonly found in most kitchens, making it easy to whip up a batch of these cupcakes at a moment's notice.

The first step is to combine the dry ingredients – flour, cocoa powder, baking soda, and salt – in a bowl and set them aside. In a separate bowl, cream the butter and sugar until light and fluffy. Add the eggs, one at a time, beating well after each addition. Then, mix in the buttermilk, vanilla extract, and red food coloring, creating a vibrant red batter.

Next, gradually add the dry ingredients to the wet mixture, mixing until just combined. Be careful not to overmix, as it can result in a dense cupcake. Once the batter is ready, scoop it into lined cupcake tins, filling each about two-thirds full. Bake the cupcakes in a preheated oven until a toothpick inserted into the center comes out clean.

While the cupcakes cool, prepare the cream cheese frosting. This frosting is made with cream cheese, butter, powdered sugar, and vanilla extract. Beat the cream cheese and butter until smooth, then gradually add the powdered sugar and vanilla extract. Continue beating until the frosting is light and fluffy.

Once the cupcakes have cooled completely, generously spread the cream cheese frosting over the tops. For added flair, you can garnish the cupcakes with sprinkles, chocolate shavings, or a drizzle of chocolate sauce. These Red Velvet Cupcakes with Cream Cheese Frosting are sure to be a hit with anyone in your family, making them a perfect addition to your collection of holiday treats.

Whether you're baking for a special occasion or simply craving a delicious dessert, these Red Velvet Cupcakes with Cream Cheese Frosting will always be a crowd-pleaser. The timeless combination of moist red velvet cake and tangy cream cheese frosting is a match made in heaven. So, gather your loved ones, put on some holiday music, and indulge in these delectable treats that are sure to bring joy to your home.

Chapter 3: Timeless Cheesecake Recipes

New York-Style Cheesecake

When it comes to classic desserts, few can rival the indulgent and creamy delight of New York-style cheesecake. This iconic treat has become a favorite in households across America, especially during the holiday season. In this chapter, we will explore the secrets behind creating the perfect New York-style cheesecake that will leave your family and friends begging for more.

The origins of New York-style cheesecake can be traced back to the early 1900s, when immigrants from Europe brought their traditional cheesecake recipes to the bustling city. Over the years, this rich and velvety dessert has evolved into its own distinct style, characterized by its dense and smooth texture, tall stature, and a graham cracker crust.

To start our cheesecake journey, we will delve into the art of creating the perfect crust. A combination of crushed graham crackers, melted butter, and a touch of sugar is the foundation for a classic New York-style cheesecake. The crust provides a delicious contrast to the creamy filling and adds a satisfying crunch to each bite.

Next, we will explore the secrets behind achieving the signature texture of a New York-style cheesecake. The key lies in using high-quality cream cheese, eggs, and sour cream. These ingredients, when combined and baked at the right temperature and time, create a luscious and velvety filling that is rich in flavor and incredibly smooth.

We will also discuss various flavor variations that can be incorporated into our New York-style cheesecake. From classic vanilla to decadent chocolate, fruity swirls, or even a touch of caramel, the possibilities are endless. These variations allow you to personalize your cheesecake and make it a truly unforgettable dessert for any occasion.

Lastly, we will share some tips and tricks for perfecting the baking process and ensuring your cheesecake comes out flawless every time. From proper cooling techniques to preventing cracks on the surface, these insider secrets will elevate your cheesecake-making skills to new heights.

Whether you are a seasoned baker or just starting your culinary journey, this chapter on New York-style cheesecake is sure to inspire and delight. So gather your loved ones, put on your apron, and get ready to create some truly memorable holiday treats with these timeless cheesecake recipes.

Classic Graham Cracker Crust

There's something undeniably comforting and nostalgic about a classic graham cracker crust. It's the perfect foundation for a wide variety of desserts, from pies to cheesecakes. In this subchapter, we will delve into the timeless art of creating the perfect graham cracker crust that will have your family coming back for seconds.

Whether you're a seasoned baker or just starting out, this recipe is foolproof and will surely become a family favorite. The ingredients are simple and readily available in any pantry, making it a go-to crust for your holiday treats.

To begin, gather the following ingredients:

- 1 ½ cups of graham cracker crumbs
- ⅓ cup of granulated sugar
- ⅓ cup of melted butter

Start by preheating your oven to 350°F (175°C). In a mixing bowl, combine the graham cracker crumbs and granulated sugar. Stir them together until well blended. Slowly pour in the melted butter, mixing it well to ensure that all the crumbs are evenly coated.

Once the mixture is well combined, press it firmly into the bottom of a pie dish or springform pan. Make sure to evenly distribute the crust along the bottom and slightly up the sides of the dish. This will create a sturdy base for your desserts.

Next, place the crust in the preheated oven and bake for 8-10 minutes until it turns golden brown. Remove it from the oven and let it cool completely before filling it with your desired dessert filling. The crust will firm up as it cools, providing the perfect texture and flavor.

This classic graham cracker crust pairs exceptionally well with creamy cheesecakes, velvety pumpkin pies, and even fruity tarts. Its slightly sweet and buttery taste adds a delightful contrast to any filling, making it a versatile choice for all occasions.

So, whether you're celebrating a holiday or simply want to treat your family to a delicious homemade dessert, this classic graham cracker crust is a timeless choice that will never disappoint. Give it a try and watch as your loved ones indulge in the irresistible flavors that this crust brings to your favorite treats.

Creamy Vanilla Cheesecake Filling

There's something about the holiday season that calls for indulging in rich and decadent desserts. And what better way to satisfy your sweet tooth than with a luscious, homemade cheesecake? In this subchapter, we'll be exploring the tantalizing world of creamy vanilla cheesecake filling – a classic and beloved flavor that is sure to delight your family and friends during the holiday season.

Nothing beats the smooth and velvety texture of a well-made cheesecake filling. The combination of cream cheese, sugar, and vanilla extract creates a heavenly taste that is both comforting and nostalgic. Whether you're serving it as the star of the dessert table or as a delightful accompaniment to your favorite holiday treats, this creamy vanilla cheesecake filling is sure to be a crowd-pleaser.

To make this delectable filling, start by beating together cream cheese and sugar until light and fluffy. This step ensures that the filling is perfectly smooth and free of any lumps. Then, add in a generous amount of pure vanilla extract, which provides a warm and fragrant flavor that pairs beautifully with the tanginess of the cream cheese.

Once the filling is thoroughly mixed, it's time to pour it into your pre-baked crust. Whether you prefer a classic graham cracker crust or something more adventurous like a chocolate cookie crust, the creamy vanilla cheesecake filling will complement it perfectly. Smooth the filling evenly over the crust, making sure to eliminate any air bubbles for a flawless finish.

Bake the cheesecake until it's set and slightly jiggly in the center. The aroma of vanilla will fill your kitchen, creating an irresistible anticipation for the moment when you finally get to slice into this delightful dessert. Allow the cheesecake to cool completely before refrigerating it for several hours or overnight. This step is crucial for achieving the perfect creamy consistency that makes cheesecake so irresistible.

When the time comes to serve your masterpiece, don't be afraid to get creative with the presentation. Top it with fresh berries, a drizzle of caramel sauce, or a dollop of whipped cream to add an extra touch of elegance and flavor.

Whether it's a holiday gathering, a special occasion, or simply a cozy family night in, this creamy vanilla cheesecake filling is guaranteed to bring joy and satisfaction to anyone who takes a bite. So go ahead, indulge in this timeless treat and create lasting memories with your loved ones this holiday season.

Tips for Achieving the Perfect Texture

One of the most important aspects of creating delicious holiday treats and classic cheesecakes is achieving the perfect texture. Whether you're a seasoned baker or just starting out, these tips will help you create desserts that are not only visually appealing but also melt-in-your-mouth delicious.

1. Start with room temperature ingredients: Before you begin baking, make sure to bring all your ingredients, such as eggs, butter, and cream cheese, to room temperature. This ensures that they mix together smoothly and evenly, resulting in a creamy and smooth texture.

2. Use the right flour: Different recipes call for different types of flour, such as all-purpose, cake flour, or bread flour. Using the right type of flour for your recipe will help you achieve the desired texture. All-purpose flour is a safe choice for most holiday treats and cheesecakes.

3. Don't overmix the batter: When mixing the ingredients, be careful not to overmix the batter. Overmixing can lead to a tough and dense texture. Mix until the ingredients are just combined to avoid any unwanted texture issues.

4. Choose the right pan: The type of pan you use can greatly affect the texture of your dessert. For cheesecakes, a springform pan is recommended as it allows for easy removal without damaging the texture. For other treats, consider using non-stick pans or parchment paper to prevent sticking and ensure an even bake.

5. Use a water bath for cheesecakes: To achieve a smooth and creamy texture in your cheesecakes, consider using a water bath. This involves placing the cheesecake pan in a larger pan filled with hot water while baking. The steam created helps prevent cracks and ensures a moist and velvety texture.

6. Cool properly: After baking, it's crucial to cool your treats properly. For cheesecakes, allow them to cool at room temperature for a while before refrigerating. This gradual cooling helps prevent cracking and ensures a creamy texture. For other treats, ensure they are completely cooled before serving to maintain their intended texture.

By following these tips, you'll be well on your way to achieving the perfect texture in your family-favorite holiday treats and classic cheesecake recipes. Remember to experiment, have fun, and don't be afraid to try new techniques to create desserts that will delight your loved ones this holiday season.

Decadent Chocolate Cheesecake

Indulge in the ultimate chocolate lover's dream with this sinfully delicious Decadent Chocolate Cheesecake recipe. Perfect for any occasion, this rich and creamy dessert is a showstopper that will leave your taste buds begging for more. Whether it's a holiday gathering, a special family meal, or just a weekend treat, this recipe is guaranteed to impress and satisfy everyone's sweet tooth.

The crust is made from crushed chocolate cookies, adding an extra layer of chocolatey goodness to the already irresistible dessert. The velvety smooth cheesecake filling combines the luscious flavors of cream cheese, melted chocolate, and a touch of cocoa powder, creating a heavenly blend that will melt in your mouth. Topped with a decadent ganache and sprinkled with chocolate shavings, this cheesecake is truly a work of art.

What sets this Decadent Chocolate Cheesecake apart is its simplicity and versatility. With just a few basic ingredients and straightforward instructions, even novice bakers can achieve extraordinary results. The recipe can be easily adapted to suit different dietary needs, such as using gluten-free cookies for the crust or substituting dairy-free cream cheese for a vegan version. This ensures that everyone can enjoy this delectable treat, regardless of their dietary restrictions.

Whether it's served as the centerpiece of a holiday dessert table or enjoyed as a special treat on a cozy night in, this Decadent Chocolate Cheesecake is sure to bring joy and satisfaction to your family. The timeless combination of chocolate and cheesecake is a guaranteed crowd-pleaser, making it an ideal choice for any occasion. So, why not indulge in a slice of pure chocolate heaven and create lasting memories with your loved ones?

In "Holiday Delights: Family-Favorite Treats and Classic Cheesecake Recipes," you'll find this mouthwatering recipe along with many other family-favorite holiday treats and timeless dessert recipes. From traditional favorites to unique twists, this book is a treasure trove of culinary delights that will make every celebration extra special. Whether you're an experienced baker or just starting to explore the world of desserts, this book has something for everyone. So, grab your apron, preheat your oven, and get ready to create unforgettable holiday memories with these delicious treats.

Oreo Cookie Crust

One of the most versatile and beloved crusts in the world of desserts is undoubtedly the Oreo cookie crust. With its rich chocolate flavor and crispy texture, this crust is the perfect foundation for a wide variety of desserts, including cheesecakes, pies, and tarts. In this subchapter, we will explore the wonders of the Oreo cookie crust and how it can elevate your favorite holiday treats to a whole new level.

The Oreo cookie crust is incredibly easy to make, requiring only two ingredients: Oreo cookies and melted butter. Simply place the cookies in a food processor or crush them manually in a plastic bag until they turn into fine crumbs. Mix the cookie crumbs with the melted butter, press the mixture firmly into the bottom of your desired pan, and voila! You have a delectable and decadent crust ready to be filled with your favorite holiday flavors.

One of the most popular uses for an Oreo cookie crust is in classic cheesecakes. The combination of creamy, tangy cheesecake filling with the crunchy and chocolaty crust is simply irresistible. Whether you prefer a traditional New York-style cheesecake or want to experiment with flavors like pumpkin spice or peppermint, the Oreo cookie crust will provide the perfect balance and contrast to your cheesecake creation.

But the Oreo cookie crust doesn't stop at cheesecakes. It can also be used in pies and tarts, adding a delightful twist to classic holiday desserts. Imagine a silky smooth chocolate mousse pie with a crunchy Oreo crust, or a luscious lemon tart with a zesty filling nestled in an Oreo cookie embrace. The possibilities are endless, and the results are always crowd-pleasing.

Not only is the Oreo cookie crust delicious, but it also adds a touch of nostalgia to your holiday treats. The familiar taste and texture of Oreo cookies bring back fond memories of childhood and holiday gatherings with loved ones. Sharing a dessert made with an Oreo cookie crust is not only a delicious experience but also a way to connect with your family and create new holiday traditions.

So, whether you are a seasoned baker or a beginner in the kitchen, don't hesitate to try the Oreo cookie crust in your favorite holiday treats. Its simplicity, versatility, and irresistible flavor make it a perfect addition to your repertoire of family-favorite desserts. Get creative, experiment with flavors, and enjoy the delightful crunch and chocolaty goodness of the Oreo cookie crust in your next holiday delight.

Pineapple Upside Down Cheesecake

Pineapple Upside Down Cheesecake is a delightful and unique twist on two classic desserts - pineapple upside down cake and creamy cheesecake. This heavenly dessert combines the tangy sweetness of pineapple with the rich and velvety texture of cheesecake, creating a truly irresistible treat that will leave your taste buds begging for more.

In this subchapter of "Holiday Delights: Family-Favorite Treats and Classic Cheesecake Recipes," we bring you a step-by-step guide to creating this show-stopping dessert that is sure to impress your family and loved ones. Whether you're planning a special holiday gathering or simply want to indulge in a decadent treat, this recipe is perfect for anyone looking to add a touch of elegance to their dessert table.

To start, we begin by preparing the pineapple topping. Slices of juicy pineapple are caramelized with brown sugar and butter, creating a sticky and sweet layer that forms the base of our cheesecake. The pineapple is then carefully arranged in a beautiful pattern at the bottom of the cake pan, ready to be topped with our luscious cheesecake batter.

The cheesecake filling is a creamy blend of cream cheese, sugar, eggs, and vanilla extract, creating the perfect balance of flavors to complement the sweet pineapple topping. Once the batter is poured over the pineapple, the cheesecake is baked to perfection, allowing the flavors to meld together and create a heavenly dessert.

When the cheesecake is ready, it's time for the grand finale - the flip! Carefully invert the cheesecake onto a serving platter, revealing the stunning pineapple topping that will wow your family and guests. The vibrant yellow pineapple slices peeking through the creamy cheesecake are a sight to behold, a true feast for the eyes and the palate.

Serve this Pineapple Upside Down Cheesecake as a centerpiece at your next holiday gathering, and watch as your loved ones marvel at its beauty and savor each delectable bite. This recipe is a true fusion of classic flavors and timeless desserts, bringing together the best of both worlds in one unforgettable treat.

So go ahead, indulge in this family-favorite holiday delight, and create lasting memories with your loved ones. With its irresistible combination of pineapple, caramel, and creamy cheesecake, this Pineapple Upside Down Cheesecake is sure to become a cherished recipe in your collection of timeless dessert classics.

Garnishing with Chocolate Shavings

Adding a touch of elegance and indulgence to any dessert, chocolate shavings are a timeless garnish that never fails to impress. Whether you're preparing a family-favorite holiday treat or a classic cheesecake, chocolate shavings can elevate your creation to a whole new level. In this subchapter, we will explore the art of garnishing with chocolate shavings and discover creative ways to make your desserts truly memorable.

First and foremost, it's important to choose the right type of chocolate for shaving. Dark chocolate with at least 70% cocoa content works exceptionally well, as it provides a rich, bittersweet flavor. However, feel free to experiment with milk or white chocolate if you prefer a milder taste. Make sure to use high-quality chocolate for the best results.

To create perfect chocolate shavings, you'll need a sharp vegetable peeler or a microplane grater. Start by heating the chocolate slightly to make it easier to work with. Using a smooth, steady motion, run the peeler or grater along the edge of the chocolate bar, creating thin, delicate shavings. Be careful not to apply too much pressure, as this may cause the chocolate to break or crumble.

Now, let's explore some creative ways to use chocolate shavings as a garnish. For a classic touch, sprinkle the shavings over a slice of cheesecake or a scoop of ice cream. The contrasting textures and flavors will delight your taste buds. You can also use chocolate shavings to decorate the edges of a cake or a pie, creating a stunning visual effect.

If you're feeling adventurous, consider incorporating chocolate shavings into the dessert itself. Fold them into a mousse or a whipped cream topping for added decadence. You can even mix them into cookie dough or pancake batter for a delightful surprise. The possibilities are endless!

In conclusion, garnishing with chocolate shavings is a simple yet effective way to add a touch of elegance and flavor to your family-favorite holiday treats and classic cheesecake recipes. With a little practice and creativity, you can create stunning desserts that will impress your loved ones and make any occasion truly special. So why not indulge in the art of chocolate shavings and take your desserts to the next level?

Fruit-Topped Cheesecakes

If you're looking for the perfect dessert that combines the creamy richness of cheesecake with the refreshing sweetness of fruits, then look no further! In this subchapter, we will explore the delightful world of fruit-topped cheesecakes that are guaranteed to become your family's favorite holiday treats. These timeless recipes have been passed down through generations and are sure to bring joy and satisfaction to everyone at the table.

There is something magical about the combination of smooth, velvety cheesecake and the burst of flavor that fresh fruits bring. Whether you prefer the tartness of berries, the tropical sweetness of mangoes, or the gentle tang of citrus, you'll find a fruit-topped cheesecake that suits your taste buds and adds a festive touch to any occasion.

One classic recipe that never fails to impress is the Strawberry Swirl Cheesecake. Picture a luscious vanilla cheesecake base with a vibrant red strawberry swirl on top. It's not only a treat for the eyes but also a burst of summer flavors in every bite. This recipe is perfect for family gatherings or even as a special dessert for a romantic evening.

If you're feeling adventurous and want to wow your guests, consider the Mango Passionfruit Cheesecake. The tropical combination of creamy mango cheesecake topped with a tangy passionfruit glaze is like a vacation for your taste buds. It's an excellent choice for summer parties or when you want to transport your family to a sunny beach in the middle of winter.

For those who prefer a citrusy twist, the Lemon Blueberry Cheesecake is a must-try. The zesty lemon-infused cheesecake perfectly complements the burst of fresh blueberries on top. This dessert is a delightful balance of flavors that will leave everyone craving for more.

No matter which fruit you choose, these fruit-topped cheesecakes are a celebration of flavors and memories. They are versatile, allowing you to experiment with different combinations and create your own signature dessert. So why not gather your loved ones and embark on a journey through the world of fruit-topped cheesecakes? It's a delicious adventure that will bring joy and delight to your family for years to come.

Fresh Strawberry Cheesecake

When it comes to classic desserts, cheesecake is always a crowd-pleaser. And what better way to elevate this timeless treat than by adding the vibrant flavors of fresh strawberries? In this subchapter, we present a recipe for a tantalizing Fresh Strawberry Cheesecake that will surely become a family favorite during holiday celebrations and beyond.

The Fresh Strawberry Cheesecake is a delightful combination of smooth and creamy cheesecake filling, a buttery graham cracker crust, and a luscious layer of fresh strawberries on top. This dessert not only looks stunning but also bursts with the refreshing taste of ripe strawberries, making it the perfect treat for any occasion.

To start, we guide you through creating the perfect graham cracker crust. With just a few simple steps, you'll have a base that complements the cheesecake filling beautifully. The crust adds a delicious crunch and enhances the overall texture of the dessert.

Next, we delve into the art of making the cheesecake filling. Our recipe calls for a combination of cream cheese, sugar, eggs, and vanilla extract. We provide detailed instructions on how to achieve the perfect creamy consistency and avoid any lumps. Once baked to perfection, the cheesecake filling sets beautifully, creating a velvety smooth texture that melts in your mouth.

The pièce de résistance of this recipe is the layer of fresh strawberries that adorns the top of the cheesecake. We guide you on how to select the best strawberries, ensuring they are ripe, juicy, and bursting with flavor. You'll learn how to expertly arrange the strawberries, creating an eye-catching presentation that will impress your family and guests.

Whether you're hosting a holiday gathering or simply want to indulge in a decadent dessert, our Fresh Strawberry Cheesecake is a must-try. This family-favorite treat combines the nostalgia of a classic cheesecake with the vibrant flavors of fresh strawberries, making it a timeless and irresistible dessert.

Get ready to create a show-stopping dessert that will have everyone asking for seconds. With our step-by-step instructions and helpful tips, you'll be able to master the art of making this Fresh Strawberry Cheesecake and enjoy the sweet rewards with your loved ones.

Sweet Potato Pie Cheesecake

If you're looking for a show-stopping dessert that combines the comforting flavors of sweet potato pie and the indulgence of creamy cheesecake, then look no further than this mouthwatering Sweet Potato Pie Cheesecake. This delightful creation will surely become a new family favorite during the holiday season and beyond.

Combining the best of both worlds, this recipe takes the classic sweet potato pie to new heights by transforming it into a luscious cheesecake. The velvety smooth sweet potato filling is perfectly balanced with the richness of the cream cheese, creating a harmonious blend of flavors that will leave your taste buds begging for more.

What makes this Sweet Potato Pie Cheesecake truly exceptional is the crust. We use crushed graham crackers combined with a touch of cinnamon, which adds a delightful crunch and complements the sweet potato and cheesecake layers beautifully. The combination of textures makes every bite a heavenly experience.

To make this dessert even more irresistible, we top it with a dollop of freshly whipped cream and a sprinkle of ground cinnamon. This final touch not only adds visual appeal but also enhances the overall flavor profile, creating a dessert that is as visually stunning as it is delicious.

Whether you're hosting a holiday gathering or simply want to treat your family to a special dessert, this Sweet Potato Pie Cheesecake is sure to impress. The timeless flavors and classic combination of ingredients make it a versatile choice that can be enjoyed year-round.

So, gather your loved ones, put on your apron, and get ready to create a decadent dessert that will be remembered for years to come. This recipe is not only a celebration of holiday delights but also a testament to the joy of sharing homemade treats with family and friends.

With its irresistible flavors, stunning presentation, and the perfect blend of sweet potato pie and cheesecake, this Sweet Potato Pie Cheesecake is destined to become a cherished family tradition. Embrace the holiday spirit and create lasting memories with this delightful dessert that will leave everyone asking for seconds.

Pecan Pie Cheesecake

Pecan Pie Cheesecake: The Perfect Fusion of Holiday Delights and Classic Cheesecake

Indulge your taste buds this holiday season with a show-stopping dessert that combines two beloved classics - pecan pie and cheesecake. Our Pecan Pie Cheesecake recipe is the ultimate treat that will leave your family and friends begging for more. With its irresistible combination of creamy cheesecake and rich, caramelized pecan topping, this dessert is sure to become a family favorite.

The Pecan Pie Cheesecake starts with a buttery graham cracker crust, providing a delicious foundation for the creamy cheesecake filling. The filling itself is a velvety blend of cream cheese, sugar, and vanilla extract, creating a smooth and luscious texture that melts in your mouth. The addition of finely chopped pecans adds a delightful crunch and nutty flavor to every bite.

But what truly sets our Pecan Pie Cheesecake apart is the decadent pecan pie topping. A generous layer of gooey caramel sauce coats a mound of pecans, creating a caramelized and sticky masterpiece. As the cheesecake bakes, the flavors meld together, resulting in a heavenly combination of sweet and savory, creamy and crunchy.

This dessert is perfect for any holiday gathering or special occasion. Its stunning presentation will wow your guests, and its incredible taste will keep them coming back for seconds. Whether it's Thanksgiving, Christmas, or a simple family get-together, the Pecan Pie Cheesecake is the ultimate crowd-pleaser.

To make this dessert even more irresistible, consider serving it with a dollop of freshly whipped cream or a scoop of vanilla ice cream. The coolness of the cream or ice cream complements the warmth of the caramelized pecans and adds an extra level of indulgence.

In our book, "Holiday Delights: Family-Favorite Treats and Classic Cheesecake Recipes," we understand the importance of creating timeless and delicious desserts that bring joy to the entire family. The Pecan Pie Cheesecake is just one of the many recipes we've curated to help you create lasting memories during the holiday season.

So, gather your loved ones, head to the kitchen, and let the sweet aroma of our Pecan Pie Cheesecake fill your home. Get ready to embark on a culinary journey that combines the best of both worlds - the beloved pecan pie and the timeless cheesecake. It's time to savor the magic of the holiday season, one delightful bite at a time.

Chapter 4: Classic Dessert Recipes

Homemade Apple Crisp

There's nothing quite like the aroma of freshly baked apple crisp wafting through the house during the holiday season. This classic dessert is a favorite among families, and it's easy to see why. With its warm, cinnamon-spiced apples and crunchy oat topping, homemade apple crisp is the perfect treat to enjoy with loved ones on a cozy winter evening.

In this subchapter, we delve into the world of homemade apple crisp, sharing our family-favorite recipe and tips for creating the perfect dessert. Whether you're a seasoned baker or just starting out, this recipe is sure to become a staple in your holiday repertoire.

To start, you'll need a few simple ingredients that are likely already in your pantry. Fresh apples, preferably tart varieties like Granny Smith or Honeycrisp, are the star of the show. You'll also need flour, sugar, butter, cinnamon, and oats for the delicious crisp topping. Assemble these ingredients, and you're ready to get baking!

We guide you through each step of the process, from peeling and slicing the apples to mixing the crisp topping. Our recipe strikes the perfect balance between sweet and tart, and the addition of cinnamon adds a delightful warmth to the dish. As the apple crisp bakes in the oven, the apples soften and release their natural juices, creating a luscious, caramel-like sauce that pairs perfectly with the crunchy topping.

Not only is homemade apple crisp a delicious dessert, but it's also a versatile one. Serve it warm with a scoop of vanilla ice cream for a comforting treat, or enjoy it cold the next day for a delightful breakfast. You can even add a drizzle of caramel sauce or a sprinkle of chopped nuts for an extra-special touch.

In this subchapter, we also explore variations of the classic apple crisp recipe, such as adding cranberries or pears for a unique twist. We provide tips for choosing the best apples, adjusting the sweetness to your preference, and storing leftovers.

Whether you're baking for a holiday gathering or simply craving a taste of nostalgia, homemade apple crisp is a timeless dessert that will bring joy to your family's table. So grab your apron and get ready to create a mouthwatering treat that will become a cherished tradition for years to come.

Crispy Cinnamon-Spiced Apple Filling

There's nothing quite like the comforting aroma of apple pie baking in the oven during the holiday season. The combination of crisp, tart apples, warm cinnamon, and a buttery crust is a timeless favorite that has been passed down through generations. In this subchapter, we will explore a delightful twist on the classic apple pie filling – the crispy cinnamon-spiced apple filling.

This recipe is perfect for anyone looking to add a little extra flair to their holiday dessert spread. Whether you're hosting a family gathering or simply want to treat yourself to a delicious homemade treat, this apple filling will surely become a family favorite.

To start, gather the freshest, firm yet juicy apples you can find. Granny Smith or Honeycrisp apples work exceptionally well for this recipe, as their tartness balances perfectly with the sweetness of the cinnamon-spiced syrup. Peel and core the apples, then slice them into thin, even pieces.

Next, prepare the cinnamon-spiced syrup by combining brown sugar, cinnamon, nutmeg, and a pinch of salt in a saucepan. Stir in a dollop of butter and let the mixture simmer until it becomes thick and glossy. This syrup will coat the apple slices, infusing them with warm, aromatic flavors that will make your taste buds dance with delight.

Once the syrup is ready, gently toss the apple slices in the mixture until they are well coated. Place the apples in a baking dish lined with a buttery crust, creating a generous layer of the cinnamon-spiced apple filling. Cover the dish with another layer of the crust, crimping the edges to seal in the deliciousness.

Bake the pie until the crust turns golden brown and the filling starts to bubble. The aroma that fills your kitchen will be absolutely heavenly! Allow the pie to cool slightly before serving, as this will help the filling set and intensify the flavors.

Whether you serve it warm with a scoop of vanilla ice cream or enjoy it chilled with a dollop of whipped cream, this crispy cinnamon-spiced apple filling is sure to become a beloved holiday treat. Its irresistible blend of tart apples, warm spices, and buttery crust will create memories that last a lifetime. So gather your loved ones, embrace the holiday spirit, and indulge in this family-favorite dessert.

Buttery Oatmeal Crumble Topping

There's something magical about the combination of butter, oats, and sugar that creates a tantalizingly delicious topping for any dessert. Whether you're making a fruit crisp, pie, or even a creamy cheesecake, a buttery oatmeal crumble topping takes it to the next level of indulgence. In this subchapter, we will explore the secrets to creating the perfect crumble topping that will have your family and loved ones begging for seconds.

The beauty of a buttery oatmeal crumble topping lies in its simplicity. It's made with just a few basic ingredients that you probably already have in your pantry. Rolled oats provide a hearty texture, while brown sugar adds a touch of sweetness and a caramel-like flavor. And of course, no crumble topping would be complete without a generous amount of butter, which creates that irresistibly rich and buttery taste.

To make the perfect crumble topping, start by combining the oats, flour, and brown sugar in a bowl. Then, using your fingers or a pastry cutter, work the cold butter into the mixture until it resembles coarse crumbs. The key here is to keep the butter cold and not overmix, as this will result in a crumbly texture that melts in your mouth.

Once you've mastered the basic crumble topping, the possibilities are endless. Sprinkle it generously over a warm apple pie for a comforting treat that screams fall. Or use it to top a luscious berry crisp, where the buttery goodness combines with the tangy sweetness of the fruit. And let's not forget about cheesecakes! A sprinkle of this crumble topping adds a delightful crunch to creamy and velvety cheesecakes, creating a perfect balance of textures.

The best part is that this versatile crumble topping can be made in advance and stored in the refrigerator or freezer. So, when the holiday season rolls around and you're short on time, you can simply grab a batch from your freezer and sprinkle it over your favorite dessert for a homemade touch that will wow your guests.

In this subchapter, we will share some of our favorite dessert recipes that pair perfectly with a buttery oatmeal crumble topping. From classic apple crisp to decadent pumpkin cheesecake, these family-favorite holiday treats will become a staple in your festive repertoire. Get ready to embrace the comforting flavors and timeless charm of these delightful desserts!

Serving with Vanilla Ice Cream

One of the greatest pleasures during the holiday season is indulging in delicious treats and desserts that have become family traditions. Whether it's a classic cheesecake recipe or a mouth-watering holiday treat, there is one accompaniment that can take any dessert to the next level - vanilla ice cream.

Vanilla ice cream has been a favorite dessert pairing for generations. Its creamy texture and subtle sweetness perfectly complement the richness and flavors of holiday treats. Whether you're serving a warm slice of apple pie, a decadent chocolate cake, or a homemade fruit cobbler, a scoop of vanilla ice cream on top can elevate the dessert experience to new heights.

There's something magical about the contrast of warm and cold, soft and creamy, that makes serving vanilla ice cream with holiday treats a winning combination. As the ice cream starts to melt and mingle with the dessert, it creates a delightful blend of flavors and textures that is simply irresistible. The smoothness of the ice cream cuts through the richness of the dessert, providing a refreshing balance that leaves your taste buds craving for more.

Moreover, vanilla ice cream is a versatile companion that pairs well with a wide range of flavors. Its subtle taste doesn't overpower the dessert but rather enhances the existing flavors, allowing them to shine. Whether your holiday treat is fruity, chocolaty, or nutty, vanilla ice cream acts as a neutral base that ties all the flavors together, creating a harmonious symphony of taste.

Not to mention, serving vanilla ice cream adds an element of nostalgia and familiarity to the dessert experience. Many of us have fond childhood memories of enjoying a scoop of vanilla ice cream with our favorite holiday treats. By continuing this tradition and serving vanilla ice cream to your family and loved ones, you're not only treating their taste buds but also creating lasting memories that will be cherished for years to come.

So, this holiday season, when you're preparing your family-favorite treats and classic cheesecake recipes, don't forget to serve them with a generous scoop of creamy, delicious vanilla ice cream. It's the perfect finishing touch that will make your desserts truly unforgettable and bring joy and delight to everyone, young and old.

Rich Chocolate Brownies

Subchapter: Rich Chocolate Brownies

Introduction:
Indulging in the rich, fudgy goodness of a perfectly baked chocolate brownie is one of life's greatest pleasures. In this subchapter, we bring you a timeless recipe for rich chocolate brownies that will have your taste buds dancing with delight. Whether you're baking for a holiday gathering or simply craving a decadent treat for yourself and your family, these brownies are a guaranteed hit. Get ready to experience a symphony of chocolate flavors in every bite!

Recipe: Rich Chocolate Brownies

Ingredients:
- 1 cup unsalted butter
- 2 cups granulated sugar
- 4 large eggs
- 1 teaspoon pure vanilla extract
- 1 cup all-purpose flour
- 1/2 cup unsweetened cocoa powder
- 1/2 teaspoon salt
- 1 cup chocolate chips

Instructions:

1. Preheat your oven to 350°F (175°C) and grease a 9x13-inch baking dish.

2. In a microwave-safe bowl, melt the butter. Add sugar and stir until well combined.

3. Add the eggs, one at a time, beating well after each addition. Stir in the vanilla extract.

4. In a separate bowl, whisk together the flour, cocoa powder, and salt. Gradually add the dry ingredients to the wet mixture, stirring until just combined. Be careful not to overmix.

5. Fold in the chocolate chips, ensuring they are evenly distributed throughout the batter.

6. Pour the batter into the prepared baking dish, spreading it out evenly.

7. Bake for 25-30 minutes or until a toothpick inserted into the center comes out with a few moist crumbs.

8. Allow the brownies to cool completely before cutting into squares and serving.

Conclusion:

These rich chocolate brownies are a timeless family-favorite treat that will bring joy to any holiday gathering. The combination of buttery richness, deep chocolate flavor, and the perfect fudgy texture makes them irresistibly delicious. Whether you enjoy them on their own or with a scoop of vanilla ice cream, these brownies are sure to become a beloved dessert in your household. So grab your apron, preheat your oven, and get ready to create a batch of these indulgent brownies that will leave your loved ones asking for more. Happy baking and enjoy the delightful moments these brownies bring to your family!

Fudgy Chocolate Brownie Batter

There's nothing quite like the irresistible aroma of freshly baked brownies wafting through the kitchen. The rich, fudgy texture and intense chocolate flavor make them a beloved treat for people of all ages. In this subchapter, we dive into the art of creating the ultimate fudgy chocolate brownie batter that will leave your taste buds dancing with delight.

Whether you're preparing for a festive holiday gathering or simply want to indulge in a decadent dessert at home, this recipe is a must-try. The secret to achieving the perfect fudgy texture lies in the careful balance of ingredients and precise baking techniques, which we will guide you through step by step.

To start, gather the finest quality chocolate and cocoa powder you can find. The combination of these two ingredients will give your brownies that deep, intense chocolate flavor that will have everyone coming back for seconds. We recommend using a dark chocolate with at least 70% cocoa content for an extra rich taste.

Next, it's time to blend together the dry and wet ingredients. The key here is to mix them just until they are combined, being careful not to overmix as this can result in a cakier texture. Fold in some chopped walnuts or chocolate chips if desired, adding a delightful crunch to every bite.

Once your batter is ready, pour it into a greased baking dish and smooth the top with a spatula. To achieve that signature crackly top, bake the brownies at a slightly higher temperature for the first few minutes before reducing it for the remainder of the baking time. This will create a beautiful contrast between the crispy top and the gooey center.

Once your brownies are baked to perfection, allow them to cool slightly before cutting them into squares and serving. These fudgy chocolate brownies are the ultimate crowd-pleaser, whether enjoyed warm with a scoop of vanilla ice cream or savored as a midnight snack.

Whether you're celebrating a holiday or simply craving a delicious treat, this recipe for fudgy chocolate brownie batter is sure to become a family-favorite. Get ready to indulge in a dessert that combines the timeless appeal of chocolate with the irresistible fudginess of a classic brownie.

Adding Nuts or Chocolate Chips

In the world of desserts, there's just something irresistible about the combination of nuts or chocolate chips with our favorite treats. Whether it's a classic cheesecake or a holiday delight, the addition of these crunchy or gooey ingredients takes the flavor to a whole new level. In this subchapter, we will explore the art of enhancing your family-favorite holiday treats and timeless cheesecake recipes with the goodness of nuts or the decadence of chocolate chips.

Nuts, such as almonds, walnuts, or pecans, bring a delightful crunch and a burst of flavor to any dessert. They can be lightly toasted and sprinkled on top of a cheesecake or folded into the batter, creating a delightful surprise in every bite. The earthy and rich taste of nuts adds depth to the overall flavor profile of the dessert, making it a true crowd-pleaser. Whether you prefer the buttery goodness of pecans or the slightly bitter taste of almonds, experimenting with different nuts will keep your family coming back for more.

On the other hand, chocolate chips are a timeless addition to any dessert recipe. Whether it's dark, milk, or white chocolate, these tiny morsels of sweetness bring a touch of indulgence to your creations. You can stir them into the cheesecake batter for a gooey and melty surprise or sprinkle them generously on top, adding a delightful chocolatey crunch. The combination of creamy cheesecake and the burst of chocolate flavor is a match made in dessert heaven, a treat that will have even the pickiest eaters begging for seconds.

No matter which option you choose, adding nuts or chocolate chips to your family-favorite holiday treats and classic cheesecake recipes is a surefire way to elevate them to a whole new level. The contrasting textures and flavors create a symphony of taste that will delight everyone around the table. So, go ahead and get creative with your desserts, experimenting with different nuts or chocolate chip varieties. Your family will thank you for it, and these treats will become cherished traditions for generations to come.

Creative Variations: Mint or Peanut Butter Swirl

When it comes to family-favorite holiday treats, cheesecake is always a top contender. Its creamy texture and rich flavors make it the perfect dessert to celebrate special occasions with your loved ones. In this subchapter, we will explore two creative variations that are sure to delight your taste buds: Mint Swirl and Peanut Butter Swirl cheesecakes.

The Mint Swirl cheesecake is a refreshing twist on the classic dessert. With a velvety smooth texture and a burst of cool mint flavor, this variation is perfect for those who love the combination of chocolate and mint. The crust is made with crushed chocolate cookies and melted butter, providing a delicious base for the creamy mint filling. To achieve the beautiful swirl effect, a mint-flavored batter is gently swirled into the cheesecake mixture before baking. The result is a stunning dessert that will impress your family and friends.

On the other hand, the Peanut Butter Swirl cheesecake is a dream come true for all peanut butter lovers. The crust is made with crushed graham crackers and melted butter, providing a crunchy and buttery base for the creamy peanut butter filling. The swirl effect is achieved by drizzling melted peanut butter over the cheesecake batter and gently swirling it with a toothpick or a knife. The combination of the rich and creamy cheesecake with the nutty and slightly salty peanut butter creates a truly irresistible dessert that will have everyone coming back for seconds.

Both variations can be decorated with chocolate shavings, whipped cream, or a drizzle of chocolate sauce for an extra touch of indulgence. These creative variations are perfect for any holiday gathering or special occasion, as they add a unique twist to the classic cheesecake recipe.

Whether you choose the refreshing Mint Swirl or the indulgent Peanut Butter Swirl, these creative variations are guaranteed to become family favorites. The combination of flavors and textures in these cheesecakes will leave your taste buds craving more. So, why not surprise your loved ones this holiday season with a delicious and unique cheesecake that will surely impress? Get ready to enjoy the delightful flavors and create wonderful memories with our Mint Swirl and Peanut Butter Swirl cheesecakes.

Creamy Rice Pudding

Rice pudding is a classic dessert that has been enjoyed by families for generations. Its rich and creamy texture, combined with the subtle sweetness of the rice and the warm flavors of cinnamon and vanilla, make it a perfect treat for any occasion, especially during the holidays. In this subchapter, we will explore the secrets to creating the perfect creamy rice pudding that will delight your family and become a beloved holiday tradition.

The key to a creamy rice pudding lies in the quality of the ingredients and the cooking technique. We will start by selecting the right type of rice – Arborio or short-grain rice works best as it releases starch during cooking, resulting in a creamy texture. Next, we will simmer the rice in a mixture of milk, sugar, and vanilla, allowing the flavors to infuse into the grains. To enhance the taste, a pinch of salt and a sprinkle of cinnamon will be added, adding depth and warmth to the dish.

As the rice cooks, it will gradually absorb the liquid and become tender. To achieve a creamy consistency, we will stir the mixture frequently, ensuring that the rice does not stick to the bottom of the pan. Once the rice is fully cooked and the pudding has thickened, we will remove it from the heat and let it cool slightly. This will allow the flavors to meld together and the pudding to set.

When serving the creamy rice pudding, you can choose to enjoy it warm or chilled, depending on your preference. Some families like to top it with a dollop of whipped cream or a sprinkle of nutmeg for an extra touch of indulgence. However you choose to savor it, this timeless dessert is sure to bring joy and comfort to your loved ones during the holiday season.

In conclusion, creamy rice pudding is a family-favorite holiday treat that never goes out of style. With its velvety texture and delicate flavors, it is a dessert that appeals to everyone. Whether you serve it as a standalone dessert or as a side dish to complement your holiday feast, this recipe will surely become a cherished tradition in your family. So gather your loved ones, whip up a batch of creamy rice pudding, and create lasting memories this holiday season.

Tender Rice Cooked in Milk

Subchapter: Tender Rice Cooked in Milk

Welcome to a delightful subchapter of "Holiday Delights: Family-Favorite Treats and Classic Cheesecake Recipes." In this section, we will explore the enchanting world of Tender Rice Cooked in Milk, a timeless and comforting dessert that will surely delight your family during the holiday season.

There's something magical about the combination of tender rice and creamy milk that creates a dessert that is both simple and luxurious. Perfect for any occasion, this recipe is a family-favorite that has stood the test of time. Whether you're preparing for a festive gathering or simply craving a comforting treat, Tender Rice Cooked in Milk is guaranteed to bring smiles to your loved ones' faces.

To make this delightful dessert, you'll need some basic ingredients that are likely already in your pantry. Begin by rinsing the rice to remove any excess starch, then combine it with whole milk, sugar, a touch of vanilla extract, and a pinch of salt in a saucepan. Allow the mixture to gently simmer over low heat, stirring occasionally to prevent the rice from sticking to the bottom of the pan.

As the rice simmers, it absorbs the velvety milk, resulting in a tender and creamy texture. The gentle warmth of the milk infuses the grains with a delicate sweetness, while the vanilla extract adds a subtle hint of aromatic flavor. The scent of this dish wafting through your home will undoubtedly create a festive holiday atmosphere that your family will cherish.

Once the rice has cooked to perfection, remove it from the heat and let it cool slightly. You can serve this dessert warm or chilled, depending on your preference. For an extra touch of elegance, sprinkle some ground cinnamon or nutmeg on top before serving, adding a festive and aromatic finish to your creation.

Tender Rice Cooked in Milk is a versatile dessert that can be enjoyed on its own or paired with various toppings. Some popular choices include fresh berries, toasted nuts, or even a drizzle of caramel sauce. Get creative and let your family personalize their bowls with their favorite flavors.

Indulge in the classic allure of Tender Rice Cooked in Milk this holiday season. This family-favorite dessert is sure to become a treasured tradition, creating lasting memories for years to come. So gather your loved ones, savor the comforting flavors, and embrace the joyous spirit of the holidays with this timeless treat.

Sweetened with Sugar and Vanilla

In the world of desserts, there are few flavors as universally loved as sugar and vanilla. These two ingredients have the magical ability to transform any dish into a delectable treat that brings joy to both young and old. In this subchapter, we explore the enchanting world of sugar and vanilla as we delve into family-favorite holiday treats and timeless cheesecake and dessert recipes.

The holiday season is a time for indulgence, and what better way to celebrate than with a spread of mouthwatering treats? From classic sugar cookies to fluffy marshmallows dipped in rich chocolate, the possibilities are endless. We bring you a collection of our most beloved family recipes, passed down through generations, that are guaranteed to delight your taste buds and create lasting memories. Whether you're baking with your little ones or impressing your in-laws, these treats are sure to be a hit at any holiday gathering.

But the magic of sugar and vanilla doesn't stop there. Cheesecake, with its creamy texture and melt-in-your-mouth goodness, is the epitome of dessert perfection. We present to you a selection of timeless cheesecake recipes that have stood the test of time. From classic New York-style cheesecake to innovative variations like salted caramel and pumpkin spice, there's a cheesecake for every occasion. Each recipe is meticulously crafted to ensure a velvety smooth texture and a balanced sweetness that will leave you craving for more.

To truly master the art of dessert making, it is essential to understand the role of sugar and vanilla. Sugar not only adds sweetness but also contributes to the texture and browning of baked goods. Meanwhile, vanilla, with its delicate and aromatic flavor, enhances the overall taste profile of any dish. We provide insights into the science behind these ingredients and offer tips and tricks to help you achieve the perfect balance in your creations.

Whether you're a seasoned baker or a newbie in the kitchen, this subchapter is a treasure trove of inspiration and guidance. So grab your apron, preheat your oven, and get ready to embark on a delicious journey filled with family-favorite holiday treats and timeless cheesecake and dessert recipes. Let the aroma of sugar and vanilla fill your home and create cherished moments with your loved ones.

Optional Flavorings: Cinnamon or Nutmeg

When it comes to holiday treats and classic cheesecake recipes, nothing adds warmth and depth of flavor quite like the optional flavorings of cinnamon or nutmeg. These versatile spices have been cherished for centuries and are beloved by people of all ages. Whether you're looking to create a nostalgic family-favorite or a timeless dessert, incorporating cinnamon or nutmeg into your recipes will surely delight your loved ones.

Cinnamon, with its distinct sweet and woody aroma, is a staple in holiday baking. Its warm flavor pairs perfectly with an array of ingredients, making it a versatile addition to any recipe. Sprinkle a pinch of cinnamon on top of your cheesecake before baking, and watch it transform into a decadent masterpiece. The fragrance will permeate your kitchen, inviting everyone to gather around and indulge in the comforting flavors of the season.

Nutmeg, on the other hand, adds a subtle, yet distinctive taste to desserts. With its slightly sweet and nutty flavor, this spice is often associated with holiday traditions and memories. A sprinkle of freshly grated nutmeg on top of your cheesecake can elevate the dish to a whole new level. Its warm and earthy notes will transport you back to cherished moments spent with family and loved ones.

Whether you choose to use cinnamon or nutmeg, the possibilities are endless. Consider adding a dash of cinnamon to your graham cracker crust for an extra layer of flavor. Alternatively, a pinch of nutmeg in the cheesecake filling can create a delightful twist. These optional flavorings can be used individually or combined, depending on your personal preference. Experimenting with different ratios will allow you to create a custom taste that suits your family's unique palate.

In conclusion, cinnamon and nutmeg are beloved ingredients that bring warmth and nostalgia to any holiday dessert. These optional flavorings can transform a simple cheesecake into a cherished family favorite. Whether you choose cinnamon's sweet and woody notes or nutmeg's subtle and nutty undertones, your loved ones will be delighted by the comforting flavors of these timeless spices. So, this holiday season, embrace the magic of cinnamon and nutmeg, and create unforgettable memories with your family as you savor each delicious bite.

Chapter 5: Tips and Tricks for Successful Baking

Essential Baking Equipment

Baking is a beloved tradition that brings families together, especially during the holiday season. Whether you're a seasoned baker or a beginner in the kitchen, having the right equipment is essential to achieve the perfect results. In this subchapter, we will explore the must-have baking equipment that will help you create delectable treats and classic cheesecake recipes that your family will love.

First and foremost, a good quality oven is the heart of any baker's kitchen. Make sure your oven has accurate temperature control and even heat distribution to ensure your baked goods are cooked to perfection. Investing in an oven thermometer can also be helpful to ensure the temperature is accurate.

Next, a sturdy and reliable stand mixer is a game-changer when it comes to baking. From whipping cream to kneading dough, a stand mixer can save you time and effort. Look for a model with different speed settings and various attachments like a paddle, whisk, and dough hook.

Another essential tool is a set of measuring cups and spoons. Baking is a science, and precise measurements are crucial for successful recipes. A digital kitchen scale is also handy, especially for recipes that require ingredients to be weighed instead of measured.

A good set of mixing bowls in various sizes is also necessary. Stainless steel or glass bowls are preferred as they are easy to clean and don't absorb flavors or odors. Additionally, a silicone spatula is a versatile tool for mixing, folding, and scraping the sides of bowls.

When it comes to baking sheets, invest in heavy-duty, non-stick pans that distribute heat evenly. These are perfect for baking cookies, pastries, or roasting nuts. A wire cooling rack is also essential to allow air circulation and prevent your baked goods from becoming soggy.

To bake delightful cheesecakes, a springform pan is a must-have. This type of pan has a removable bottom and a latch on the side, making it easy to release the delicate cheesecake without damaging it. Additionally, a good quality blender or food processor will help you achieve smooth and creamy fillings.

Lastly, don't forget to stock up on parchment paper, aluminum foil, and baking mats. These items will prevent your baked goods from sticking to the pans and make cleanup a breeze.

Having the right baking equipment sets the foundation for successful holiday treats and classic cheesecake recipes. So, gather these essentials, put on your apron, and get ready to create delectable delights that will bring joy and happiness to your family this holiday season.

Ingredient Substitutions and Allergen Considerations

In the wonderful world of cooking and baking, sometimes we find ourselves missing a key ingredient or needing to make adjustments due to dietary restrictions or allergies. Fear not! This subchapter is here to guide you through the art of ingredient substitutions and help you create delightful treats that everyone in your family can enjoy.

Whether you are preparing family-favorite holiday treats or timeless cheesecake and dessert recipes, it's important to consider the dietary needs and preferences of your loved ones. By making a few simple swaps and substitutions, you can ensure that everyone at the table can savor the delicious flavors without worry.

For those who have dairy allergies or follow a vegan lifestyle, there are plenty of options to replace dairy products in your recipes. Instead of butter, you can use plant-based margarine or coconut oil. Almond milk, soy milk, or oat milk can be excellent substitutes for regular milk. When it comes to cream cheese, there are various dairy-free alternatives available that still provide a creamy texture and wonderful taste.

If you're looking to reduce the sugar content in your treats, natural sweeteners such as honey, maple syrup, or agave nectar can be used instead of refined sugar. Applesauce and mashed bananas are excellent substitutes for sugar in certain recipes, adding natural sweetness and moisture.

Another consideration is gluten-free baking. Many people with gluten sensitivities or celiac disease need to avoid wheat flour. Fortunately, there are numerous gluten-free flour blends on the market that can be used as a direct substitute in most recipes. Alternatively, you can experiment with almond flour, coconut flour, or even oats ground into flour for a unique twist.

Allergen considerations are crucial when preparing treats for family gatherings or parties. Always be mindful of common allergens such as nuts, eggs, and gluten. Label your treats clearly if they contain any allergenic ingredients and be prepared to offer alternatives for those with specific dietary needs.

Remember, the joy of baking and sharing treats lies in bringing smiles to the faces of your loved ones. By being mindful and making ingredient substitutions and allergen considerations, you can ensure that everyone can indulge in the delight of your family-favorite holiday treats, timeless cheesecake, and dessert recipes.

Troubleshooting Common Baking Issues

Baking is a beloved tradition, especially during the holiday season. There's nothing quite like the aroma of freshly baked treats wafting through the house, filling it with warmth and joy. However, as any experienced baker knows, sometimes things don't go according to plan. But fear not! In this subchapter, we will explore some common baking issues and provide you with simple solutions to ensure your holiday delights turn out perfectly every time.

1. Flat or sunken cakes: If your cakes are not rising properly or sinking in the middle, it could be due to expired baking powder or baking soda. Always check the expiration date before using them. Another possible cause is opening the oven door too early, which can cause a sudden drop in temperature. To avoid this, resist the temptation to peek until the minimum recommended baking time has passed.

2. Dry or dense baked goods: Dry or dense treats can be the result of overmixing the batter. When you overmix, you develop too much gluten, resulting in a tough texture. To prevent this, mix the ingredients just until they are combined. Additionally, using too much flour can also lead to dryness. Make sure to measure your ingredients accurately, using a kitchen scale if possible.

3. Burnt edges: If your cookies or bars have burnt edges while the center remains undercooked, it may be due to uneven heat distribution in your oven. To solve this issue, try using an oven thermometer to ensure your oven is heating accurately. You can also rotate the baking sheet halfway through the baking time to promote even browning.

4. Cracked cheesecakes: Cracks on the surface of a cheesecake can be disappointing, but they can easily be prevented. The most common cause is overbaking. To avoid this, check for doneness by gently shaking the cheesecake. The center should jiggle slightly, while the edges should be set. Another tip is to bake the cheesecake in a water bath, which helps to regulate the temperature and prevent cracks.

5. Sticking to the pan: To prevent your baked goods from sticking to the pan, make sure to properly grease and flour it before adding the batter. You can also line the pan with parchment paper for easy removal. If your cake still sticks, try running a knife around the edges while it's still warm to loosen it.

By addressing these common baking issues, you can ensure that your family-favorite holiday treats and timeless cheesecake recipes turn out perfectly every time. With a little troubleshooting and some handy tips, you'll be able to create delicious and memorable baked goods that will delight your loved ones. Happy baking!

Decorative Presentation Ideas for Holiday Delights

The holiday season is a time for family, joy, and of course, delicious treats! In this subchapter, we will explore some creative and festive ways to present your holiday delights. Whether you are hosting a family gathering or simply want to add a touch of whimsy to your dessert table, these decorative presentation ideas will surely delight both young and old.

1. Gingerbread Village Display: Create a charming gingerbread village as the centerpiece for your dessert table. Use gingerbread cookies to build houses, trees, and even a little gingerbread family. Dust the village with powdered sugar to resemble freshly fallen snow. Not only will it look adorable, but it will also tempt everyone to try a piece of the gingerbread goodness.

2. Festive Fruit Kabobs: Give your fruit platter a holiday makeover by turning it into festive fruit kabobs. Thread colorful fruits like strawberries, kiwis, and grapes onto skewers and arrange them in a Christmas tree shape. Place a star-shaped slice of pineapple on top for a finishing touch. This healthy and eye-catching treat will be a hit among both kids and adults.

3. Santa Hat Cupcakes: Transform ordinary cupcakes into adorable Santa hats. Frost each cupcake with a swirl of red icing and top it off with a small marshmallow. Place a trimmed strawberry on top of the marshmallow to create Santa's hat. These cute and tasty treats will add a cheerful touch to your dessert table.

4. Cheesecake Snowflakes: Use a snowflake-shaped cookie cutter to create decorative shapes from your classic cheesecake. Place the snowflake-shaped cheesecakes on a platter dusted with powdered sugar, and voila! You have a stunning and elegant dessert that captures the beauty of the winter season.

5. Hot Chocolate Bar: Set up a DIY hot chocolate bar for your guests to enjoy. Provide various toppings such as whipped cream, marshmallows, crushed candy canes, and chocolate shavings. Display festive mugs and stirring spoons to add to the holiday spirit. This interactive and cozy setup will warm both hearts and taste buds.

Remember, the presentation of your holiday delights is just as important as their taste. By incorporating these decorative ideas into your dessert table, you can create a magical and inviting atmosphere for your family and guests. Let your creativity shine and watch as everyone's eyes light up with delight as they indulge in these festive treats.

Chapter 6: Conclusion and Final Thoughts

Celebrating the Delights of Family-Favorite Treats

In the book "Holiday Delights: Family-Favorite Treats and Classic Cheesecake Recipes," we invite you to embark on a journey filled with the joy of preparing and sharing delicious treats with your loved ones. This subchapter, titled "Celebrating the Delights of Family-Favorite Treats," is dedicated to the heartwarming experience of creating and enjoying these delectable goodies together.

Family-Favorite Holiday Treats:

The holiday season is a time of warmth, love, and cherished traditions. What better way to celebrate than by indulging in family-favorite holiday treats that have been passed down through generations? From grandma's secret recipe for gingerbread cookies to dad's famous pecan pie, these treats bring back memories and create new ones. Discover the joy of baking together, sharing stories, and creating lasting bonds over these delightful confections.

Timeless Cheesecake and Dessert Recipes:

Cheesecake, the epitome of indulgence and elegance, has stood the test of time as a beloved dessert. In this subchapter, we delve into timeless cheesecake recipes that have been perfected over the years. From classic New York-style cheesecake to innovative variations like pumpkin spice or chocolate swirl, these recipes are sure to please even the most discerning palates.

But our book doesn't stop at cheesecake alone. We also offer a selection of dessert recipes that complement your holiday menu perfectly. From rich chocolate mousse to tangy lemon bars, these desserts are guaranteed to satisfy any sweet tooth. Whether you're hosting a festive dinner or simply craving a treat after a long day, these recipes will always be there to bring a smile to your face.

Creating Memories:

At its core, "Holiday Delights" is about more than just recipes. It's about creating memories and celebrating the moments that matter. Through the art of baking and cooking together, we invite you to slow down, savor the process, and embrace the joy of spending quality time with your loved ones.

So, whether you're a seasoned baker or a novice in the kitchen, "Holiday Delights" is the perfect companion for your culinary adventures. Let the delights of family-favorite treats and timeless cheesecake recipes fill your home with warmth and love this holiday season. Start creating memories that will be treasured for years to come.

Creating Lasting Memories with Classic Cheesecake Recipes

There's something magical about the holidays - the enchanting decorations, the joyful music, and of course, the delicious treats that bring families together. In "Holiday Delights: Family-Favorite Treats and Classic Cheesecake Recipes," we delve into the world of timeless cheesecake and dessert recipes, aiming to help you create lasting memories with your loved ones.

Cheesecake has always been a crowd-pleaser, a dessert that transcends generations and brings people closer. In this subchapter, we explore the art of making classic cheesecake recipes that will become cherished family traditions. Whether you're a seasoned baker or a novice in the kitchen, our recipes are designed to be easy to follow, ensuring that everyone can participate in the joy of creating these delectable treats.

Imagine the smiles on your family's faces as they gather around the table, eager to indulge in a slice of creamy, velvety cheesecake. From the traditional New York-style cheesecake to the decadent chocolate swirl or the fruity strawberry cheesecake, our recipes cater to various tastes and preferences, offering something for everyone.

But it's not just about the end result; it's about the process of creating these desserts together. The act of gathering ingredients, measuring, mixing, and baking becomes a shared experience, fostering connection and strengthening bonds. These moments spent in the kitchen will be cherished memories that you and your loved ones will look back on for years to come.

As you embark on your cheesecake-making journey, don't forget to involve the younger members of your family. Encourage them to join in the fun, teaching them the secrets of the perfect cheesecake while creating an opportunity for them to learn valuable skills. These traditions will be passed down from generation to generation, ensuring that the love for classic cheesecake lives on.

So, whether you're celebrating a special occasion or simply want to create a sweet treat to enjoy with your family, our classic cheesecake recipes will help you make memories that will be treasured for a lifetime. Let the aroma of freshly baked cheesecake fill your home, as laughter and joy permeate the air. Together, let's create lasting memories with these timeless desserts that will bring your family closer and make the holiday season even more magical.

Encouragement to Explore and Experiment in the Kitchen

Cooking is an art that allows us to express our creativity and bring joy to our loved ones. In the kitchen, we have the opportunity to explore new flavors, experiment with various techniques, and create delicious masterpieces that become family favorites. This subchapter aims to inspire anyone, especially families, to step into the kitchen with confidence and embark on a culinary adventure that will be filled with holiday delights.

The kitchen is a magical place where traditions are passed down from generation to generation. It is a space where memories are created, and family bonds are strengthened. By encouraging exploration and experimentation, we open ourselves up to new possibilities and redefine the boundaries of what is possible in the kitchen.

One of the key aspects of this subchapter is the focus on family-favorite holiday treats. These are the recipes that have stood the test of time and have become an integral part of our family gatherings. From grandma's famous apple pie to dad's secret gingerbread cookies, these treats hold a special place in our hearts. This subchapter will not only provide you with the recipes but also encourage you to add your own unique twist to these classics. After all, the best recipes are the ones that are passed down and improved upon with each generation.

In addition to holiday treats, this subchapter will also introduce you to the timeless art of cheesecake making. Cheesecake is a dessert that has been enjoyed for centuries and has evolved into countless variations. From creamy New York-style cheesecake to fruity and refreshing flavors, the possibilities are endless. By experimenting with different ingredients and techniques, you can create your own signature cheesecake that will become a staple at your family gatherings.

Whether you are a seasoned chef or a beginner in the kitchen, this subchapter is designed to inspire and empower you to explore and experiment. Through step-by-step instructions, helpful tips, and personal anecdotes, Holiday Delights: Family-Favorite Treats and Classic Cheesecake Recipes will guide you on your culinary journey. So gather your loved ones, turn up the holiday tunes, and let the magic of the kitchen unfold as you create unforgettable holiday treats and timeless cheesecake delights.

Appendix: Recipe Index with Measurements

In this appendix, you will find a comprehensive recipe index with measurements for all the delicious treats and classic cheesecake recipes featured in "Holiday Delights: Family-Favorite Treats and Classic Cheesecake Recipes." Whether you are a seasoned baker or a novice in the kitchen, this index will be your go-to resource for creating mouthwatering dishes that will impress your loved ones during the holiday season and beyond.

Family-Favorite Holiday Treats:
1. Grandma's Gingerbread Cookies - 2 cups all-purpose flour, 1 teaspoon baking soda, 1 teaspoon ground ginger, 1 teaspoon ground cinnamon, 1/2 teaspoon ground cloves, 1/2 teaspoon salt, 1/2 cup unsalted butter, 1/2 cup granulated sugar, 1/2 cup molasses, 1 large egg.
2. Auntie's Pumpkin Pie - 1 1/2 cups canned pumpkin puree, 1 cup evaporated milk, 3/4 cup granulated sugar, 1/2 teaspoon salt, 1 teaspoon ground cinnamon, 1/2 teaspoon ground ginger, 1/4 teaspoon ground cloves, 2 large eggs, 1 unbaked pie crust.
3. Mom's Classic Sugar Cookies - 2 3/4 cups all-purpose flour, 1 teaspoon baking soda, 1/2 teaspoon baking powder, 1 cup unsalted butter, 1 1/2 cups granulated sugar, 1 large egg, 1 teaspoon vanilla extract.

Timeless Cheesecake and Dessert Recipes:
1. New York Style Cheesecake - 2 cups graham cracker crumbs, 1/2 cup unsalted butter, 2 cups cream cheese, 1 cup granulated sugar, 1 teaspoon vanilla extract, 4 large eggs, 1 cup sour cream.
2. Triple Chocolate Brownies - 1 cup unsalted butter, 2 cups granulated sugar, 4 large eggs, 1 teaspoon vanilla extract, 1 cup all-purpose flour, 1/2 cup unsweetened cocoa powder, 1/4 teaspoon salt, 1 cup semisweet chocolate chips, 1 cup white chocolate chips, 1 cup milk chocolate chips.
3. Strawberry Shortcake - 2 cups all-purpose flour, 1/4 cup granulated sugar, 1 tablespoon baking powder, 1/2 teaspoon salt, 1/2 cup unsalted butter, 2/3 cup milk, 2 cups fresh strawberries, 1 cup whipped cream.

This recipe index is designed to provide you with easy access to all the recipes featured in the book. Each recipe includes precise measurements for the ingredients to ensure consistent and delicious results every time you prepare these family-favorite holiday treats or timeless cheesecake and dessert recipes.

Whether you are looking to carry on treasured family traditions or create new ones, "Holiday Delights: Family-Favorite Treats and Classic Cheesecake Recipes" has something for everyone. With this comprehensive recipe index, you can easily navigate through the book and find the perfect recipe to satisfy your cravings and delight your loved ones.

So, gather your ingredients, put on your apron, and let the magic of the holiday season fill your kitchen as you create these delectable delights. Happy baking!

Acknowledgments

Writing this book, "Holiday Delights: Family-Favorite Treats and Classic Cheesecake Recipes," has been a labor of love and would not have been possible without the support and contributions of many individuals. I would like to take this opportunity to express my deepest gratitude to everyone who has played a part in bringing this book to life.

Firstly, I want to thank my family for their unwavering support and encouragement throughout this journey. Your love and belief in me have been the driving force behind this project. Thank you for always being there to taste-test countless recipes and provide valuable feedback.

A special thank you goes to the entire team at our family kitchen. To my kids, who have spent endless hours in the kitchen with me, your enthusiasm and creativity have shaped the recipes in this book. Each one of you has brought a unique perspective and contributed immensely to the success of this project.

I would also like to extend my gratitude to the experts and chefs whose work has inspired and influenced my own culinary style. Your dedication to the craft and passion for creating delectable treats has been instrumental in shaping the content of this book. Thank you for sharing your knowledge and expertise with the world.

To my friends and beta readers, thank you for providing valuable feedback on the recipes and offering suggestions for improvement. Your honest opinions have helped refine the recipes and make them more accessible to our readers.

Lastly, I want to express my heartfelt appreciation to the readers of this book. Your love for family-favorite holiday treats and timeless cheesecake and dessert recipes has driven me to create this compilation. I hope that the recipes in this book bring joy and delight to your family gatherings, just as they have for mine.

In conclusion, I am immensely grateful to everyone who has contributed to the creation of this book. Your support, feedback, and love have been invaluable. I hope that "Holiday Delights: Family-Favorite Treats and Classic Cheesecake Recipes" becomes a cherished addition to your culinary repertoire and brings warmth and happiness to your holiday celebrations for years to come.

Thank you all from the bottom of my heart.

With love,

Kandice Merrick

These instructions should help you create these delicious dessert variations. Enjoy your baking!

Traditional Christmas Cookies:
1. In a large mixing bowl, cream together 1 cup of softened butter and 1 cup of granulated sugar until light and fluffy. 2. Beat in 2 eggs and 2 teaspoons of vanilla extract. 3. Gradually add 3 cups of all-purpose flour, 1/2 teaspoon of baking powder, and 1/4 teaspoon of salt. Mix until a dough forms. 4. Divide the dough into manageable portions and roll it out on a floured surface. 5. Use holiday-themed cookie cutters to cut out shapes and transfer them to a baking sheet. 6. Bake at 350°F (175°C) for 8-10 minutes or until the edges are lightly golden. 7. Allow the cookies to cool completely before decorating with icing, sprinkles, and other festive decorations.

Sugar Cookies with Festive Decorations: These are similar to traditional Christmas cookies but with a focus on decorating with colorful icing, sprinkles, and other decorations.

Gingerbread People and Houses:
 1. In a large mixing bowl, combine 3 cups of all-purpose flour, 1 1/2 teaspoons of ground ginger, 1 1/2 teaspoons of ground cinnamon, 1/2 teaspoon of ground cloves, 1/2 teaspoon of baking soda, and 1/2 teaspoon of salt. 2. In a separate bowl, cream together 1/2 cup of softened butter and 1/2 cup of brown sugar. 3. Add 1 egg and 1/3 cup of molasses to the butter-sugar mixture and mix well. 4. Gradually add the dry ingredients to the wet ingredients, mixing until a dough forms. 5. Divide the dough into portions, wrap in plastic wrap, and refrigerate for at least 1 hour. 6. Preheat your oven to 350°F (175°C). 7. Roll out the dough on a floured surface and use gingerbread people or house-shaped cookie cutters. 8. Bake for 10-12 minutes or until the cookies are firm but not hard. 9. Allow the cookies to cool completely, then decorate with royal icing, candies, and other decorations.

Peppermint Candy Cane Cookies:
 1. In a large mixing bowl, cream together 1 cup of softened butter and 1 cup of granulated sugar. 2. Add 2 teaspoons of peppermint extract and 1 egg, mixing until well combined. 3. Gradually add 2 1/2 cups of all-purpose flour and a pinch of salt, mixing until a dough forms. 4. Divide the dough in half, adding red food coloring to one half to create a red dough. 5. Take a small piece of each dough and roll them into ropes. 6. Twist the red and white ropes together to form candy cane shapes. 7. Bake at 375°F (190°C) for about 8 minutes. 8. While they're still warm, sprinkle crushed peppermint candy canes on top.

Pecan Pie with Buttery Crust:

For the Pie Crust:
1. In a mixing bowl, combine 1 1/4 cups of all-purpose flour and a pinch of salt. 2. Add 1/2 cup (1 stick) of cold, diced unsalted butter and mix until the mixture resembles coarse crumbs. 3. Gradually add 2-4 tablespoons of ice-cold water and mix until the dough comes together. 4. Shape the dough into a disk, wrap in plastic, and refrigerate for at least 30 minutes.

For the Pecan Filling:
5. Preheat your oven to 350°F (175°C). 6. In a separate bowl, whisk together 1 cup of corn syrup, 1 cup of granulated sugar, 3 eggs, 2 tablespoons of melted butter, and 1 teaspoon of vanilla extract. 7. Stir in 1 1/2 cups of pecan halves. 8. Roll out the pie crust and fit it into a pie dish. 9. Pour the pecan filling into the crust. 10. Bake for about 50-60 minutes or until the filling is set. 11. Allow the pie to cool before serving.

Apple Pie with Cinnamon Streusel Topping:

For the Pie Filling:
1. Peel, core, and slice 6-7 medium apples (e.g., Granny Smith or Honeycrisp). 2. In a large bowl, combine the sliced apples with 3/4 cup of granulated sugar, 2 tablespoons of all-purpose flour, 1 teaspoon of ground cinnamon, and a pinch of salt. 3. Mix well and set aside.

For the Streusel Topping:
4. In a separate bowl, combine 3/4 cup of all-purpose flour, 1/2 cup of granulated sugar, 1/2 cup of cold butter (cut into small pieces), and 1 teaspoon of cinnamon. 5. Use a pastry cutter or your hands to blend the mixture until it forms a crumbly texture.

Assembling and Baking:
6. Preheat your oven to 425°F (220°C). 7. Roll out a pie crust and fit it into a pie dish. 8. Pour the apple filling into the pie crust. 9. Sprinkle the streusel topping evenly over the apples. 10. Cover the edges of the pie with foil or a pie shield to prevent over-browning. 11. Bake for 45-55 minutes or until the crust is golden and the filling is bubbling. 12. Allow the pie to cool before serving.

Strawberry Shortcake with Whipped Cream:

For the Shortcake:
1. Preheat your oven to 425°F (220°C). 2. In a mixing bowl, combine 2 cups of all-purpose flour, 1/4 cup of granulated sugar, 1 tablespoon of baking powder, and 1/2 teaspoon of salt. 3. Add 1/2 cup (1 stick) of cold, diced butter and mix until the mixture resembles coarse crumbs. 4. Stir in 2/3 cup of milk to form a dough. 5. Drop spoonful's of dough onto a baking sheet and bake for 12-15 minutes or until golden brown. 6. Allow the shortcakes to cool.

For the Whipped Cream:
7. Whip 1 cup of heavy cream with 2 tablespoons of powdered sugar and 1 teaspoon of vanilla extract until stiff peaks form.

Assembly:
8. Slice the shortcakes in half horizontally. 9. Spoon fresh sliced strawberries onto the bottom half. 10. Top with a dollop of whipped cream and place the top half of the shortcake on top. 11. Add more whipped cream and strawberry slices as desired.

Red Velvet Cupcakes with Cream Cheese Frosting:

For the Cupcakes:
1. Preheat your oven to 350°F (175°C). 2. In a mixing bowl, cream together 1/2 cup of softened butter and 1 1/2 cups of granulated sugar. 3. Add 2 eggs and 2 tablespoons of cocoa powder mixed with red food coloring (as desired) to create a deep red color. 4. In a separate bowl, combine 2 1/2 cups of all-purpose flour and 1 teaspoon of baking powder. 5. Add the dry ingredients to the wet ingredients, alternating with 1 cup of buttermilk, starting and ending with the dry ingredients. 6. Stir in 1 teaspoon of vanilla extract and 1 tablespoon of white vinegar. 7. Spoon the batter into cupcake liners and bake for 18-20 minutes. 8. Let the cupcakes cool completely.

For the Cream Cheese Frosting:
9. In a mixing bowl, beat 8 ounces of cream cheese and 1/2 cup of butter until smooth. 10. Gradually add 4 cups of powdered sugar and 1 teaspoon of vanilla extract. Beat until creamy and smooth. 11. Frost the cooled cupcakes as desired.

New York-Style Cheesecake with Classic Graham Cracker Crust:

For the Graham Cracker Crust:
1. Preheat your oven to 325°F (160°C). 2. In a bowl, crush 1 1/2 cups of graham crackers (about 12 sheets) into fine crumbs. 3. Mix in 1/4 cup of granulated sugar. 4. Melt 1/2 cup (1 stick) of unsalted butter and add it to the crumbs. Stir until the crumbs are evenly coated. 5. Press the mixture into the bottom of a 9-inch springform pan to create the crust. 6. Bake for 10 minutes, then remove from the oven and set aside.

For the Cheesecake Filling:
7. In a large bowl, beat 4 packages (8 ounces each) of cream cheese until smooth. 8. Add 1 1/4 cups of granulated sugar and beat until well combined. 9. Mix in 1 teaspoon of vanilla extract. 10. Add 4 large eggs, one at a time, mixing well after each addition. 11. Pour the cream cheese mixture over the graham cracker crust. 12. Bake in the preheated oven for about 50-60 minutes or until the edges are set but the center still jiggles slightly. 13. Turn off the oven and leave the cheesecake inside for an additional hour. 14. Refrigerate the cheesecake for several hours or overnight before serving.

Decadent Chocolate Cheesecake:

1. Follow the same steps for making the graham cracker crust as described above. 2. For the chocolate cheesecake filling, melt 8 ounces of semi-sweet chocolate and let it cool slightly. 3. In a large bowl, combine 4 packages of cream cheese, 1 1/4 cups of granulated sugar, and 1 teaspoon of vanilla extract, as described in the New York-Style Cheesecake instructions. 4. Add the melted chocolate to the cream cheese mixture and mix well. 5. Add 4 large eggs, one at a time, mixing thoroughly after each addition. 6. Pour the chocolate cheesecake filling over the graham cracker crust and bake as directed in the New York-Style Cheesecake instructions.

Oreo Cookie Crust:

1. Crush 24 Oreo cookies into fine crumbs. 2. Mix in 1/4 cup of melted butter until the crumbs are evenly coated. 3. Press the mixture into the bottom of the springform pan instead of the graham cracker crust. You can use the same cheesecake filling from the New York-Style Cheesecake or the Decadent Chocolate Cheesecake as desired.

Pineapple Upside Down Cheesecake:

1. Prepare the graham cracker crust as in the New York-Style Cheesecake instructions. 2. In the bottom of the springform pan, arrange pineapple rings and maraschino cherries. 3. Pour a layer of caramel sauce over the fruit. 4. Prepare the cheesecake filling according to the New York-Style Cheesecake instructions. 5. Pour the cream cheese mixture over the fruit and caramel. 6. Bake and cool as directed in the New York-Style Cheesecake instructions. 7. When you remove the cheesecake from the pan, the pineapple and cherries should be on top, creating a pineapple upside-down effect.

Sweet Potato Pie Cheesecake:

1. Create a graham cracker crust as described in the New York-Style Cheesecake instructions. 2. For the cheesecake filling, combine 4 packages of cream cheese, 1 1/4 cups of sugar, 1 teaspoon of vanilla extract, and 1 1/2 cups of mashed sweet potatoes (cooked and cooled). 3. Mix in 1 teaspoon of cinnamon and 1/2 teaspoon of nutmeg. 4. Follow the baking and cooling instructions from the New York-Style Cheesecake.

Pecan Pie Cheesecake:

1. Prepare a graham cracker crust as described in the New York-Style Cheesecake instructions. 2. Create a pecan pie-inspired filling by mixing 4 packages of cream cheese, 1 1/4 cups of sugar, 1 teaspoon of vanilla extract, and 1/2 cup of light corn syrup. 3. Stir in 1 1/2 cups of chopped pecans. 4. Follow the baking and cooling instructions from the New York-Style Cheesecake.

Homemade Apple Crisp:

For the Apple Filling:
1. Preheat your oven to 350°F (175°C). 2. Peel, core, and slice 4-5 apples (e.g., Granny Smith or Honeycrisp). 3. In a bowl, toss the apple slices with 1/2 cup of granulated sugar, 1 teaspoon of ground cinnamon, and a pinch of salt. 4. Transfer the spiced apple mixture to a baking dish.

For the Oatmeal Crumble Topping:

5. In another bowl, combine 1 cup of old-fashioned rolled oats, 1/2 cup of all-purpose flour, 1/2 cup of brown sugar, and 1/2 cup (1 stick) of melted butter. 6. Mix until the ingredients are crumbly. Assembling and Baking: 7. Sprinkle the oatmeal crumble topping evenly over the apple filling. 8. Bake for 30-35 minutes or until the topping is golden brown, and the apples are tender. 9. Serve the apple crisp warm, ideally with a scoop of vanilla ice cream.

Crispy Cinnamon-Spiced Apple Filling:

1. Follow the instructions for the apple filling as described above. Buttery Oatmeal Crumble Topping: 2. Follow the oatmeal crumble topping instructions as provided in the Homemade Apple Crisp section. Serve with Vanilla Ice Cream: 3. Once your dessert (e.g., apple crisp) is ready, serve it in individual portions and top each serving with a scoop of vanilla ice cream. Enjoy the combination of hot and cold, crispy and creamy!

Rich Chocolate Brownies:

1. Preheat your oven to 350°F (175°C). 2. In a microwave-safe bowl, melt 1 cup of unsalted butter and 2 cups of sugar together. 3. Stir in 1 teaspoon of vanilla extract. 4. Mix in 4 large eggs, one at a time, until well incorporated. 5. In a separate bowl, combine 2/3 cup of unsweetened cocoa powder, 1 cup of all-purpose flour, and 1/2 teaspoon of baking powder. 6. Gradually add the dry ingredients to the wet ingredients, mixing until just combined. 7. Optionally, fold in 1 cup of chocolate chips or chopped nuts. 8. Pour the brownie batter into a greased 9x13-inch baking pan. 9. Bake for 30-35 minutes or until a toothpick inserted into the center comes out with a few moist crumbs. 10. Let the brownies cool before cutting them into squares.

Fudgy Chocolate Brownie Batter: For a fudgier texture, reduce the amount of flour to 3/4 cup in the Rich Chocolate Brownies recipe.

Creative Variations:

Mint or Peanut Butter Swirl: 12. To create a mint or peanut butter swirl, prepare the brownie batter as described in the Rich Chocolate Brownies section. 13. Pour half of the batter into the baking pan. 14. Add mint or peanut butter flavoring to the other half of the batter and mix well. 15. Alternatively drop spoonfuls of the flavored batter over the plain batter in the pan. 16. Use a knife to create a marbled effect by swirling the two batters together. 17. Bake as directed in the Rich Chocolate Brownies instructions.

Creamy Rice Pudding:

1. In a saucepan, combine 1 cup of rice, 4 cups of milk, 1/2 cup of sugar, 1/4 teaspoon of salt, and 1 teaspoon of vanilla extract. 2. Cook over medium heat, stirring frequently, until the rice is tender, and the mixture thickens (about 25-30 minutes). 3. Remove from heat and stir in 2 tablespoons of butter. 4. Let the rice pudding cool slightly and serve warm.

New Orleans Style Bread Pudding:

1. Preheat your oven to 350°F (175°C). 2. In a large bowl, tear 4-5 cups of stale bread (e.g., French bread) into small pieces. 3. In a separate bowl, whisk together 2 cups of milk, 2/3 cup of granulated sugar, 3 beaten eggs, 1/4 cup of melted butter, 1 teaspoon of vanilla extract, and a pinch of ground cinnamon.

4. Pour the mixture over the torn bread and let it sit for about 15 minutes to allow the bread to absorb the liquid. 5. Transfer the mixture to a greased baking dish. 6. Bake for 45-55 minutes or until the top is golden and the pudding is set. 7. Serve warm, optionally topped with a whiskey or rum sauce.

Enjoy making and savoring these delightful desserts!

RECIPE:

DIFFICULTY:

RATING:

PREP TIME:

COOK TIME:

INGREDIENTS:

COOKING INSTRUCTIONS:

NOTES:

RECIPE:

DIFFICULTY:

RATING:

PREP TIME:

COOK TIME:

INGREDIENTS:

COOKING INSTRUCTIONS:

NOTES:

RECIPE:

DIFFICULTY:

RATING:

PREP TIME:

COOK TIME:

INGREDIENTS:

COOKING INSTRUCTIONS:

NOTES:

RECIPE:

DIFFICULTY:

RATING:

PREP TIME:

COOK TIME:

INGREDIENTS:

COOKING INSTRUCTIONS:

NOTES: